From virtue to venality

MANCHESTER
1824

Manchester University Press

From virtue to venality

Corruption in the city

Peter Jones

Manchester University Press
Manchester and New York

distributed in the United States exclusively by Palgrave Macmillan

The right of Peter Jones to be identified as the author of this work has been asserted by him in accordance with the Copyright, Designs and Patents Act 1988.

Published by Manchester University Press
Oxford Road, Manchester M13 9NR, UK
and Room 400, 175 Fifth Avenue, New York, NY 10010, USA
www.manchesteruniversitypress.co.uk

Distributed in the United States exclusively by
Palgrave Macmillan, 175 Fifth Avenue, New York,
NY 10010, USA

Distributed in Canada exclusively by
UBC Press, University of British Columbia, 2029 West Mall,
Vancouver, BC, Canada V6T 1Z2

British Library Cataloguing-in-Publication Data
A catalogue record for this book is available from the British Library

Library of Congress Cataloging-in-Publication Data applied for

ISBN 978 0 7190 08872 8 hardback

First published 2013

The publisher has no responsibility for the persistence or accuracy of URLs for any external or third-party internet websites referred to in this book, and does not guarantee that any content on such websites is, or will remain, accurate or appropriate.

Typeset
by SPi Publisher Services, Pondicherry, India
Printed in Great Britain
by CPI Antony Rowe Ltd, Chippenham, Wiltshire

Contents

Figures

Acknowledgements

This book although short has incurred many debts. I would like to thank the University of Leicester and Professor Rosemary Sweet for supporting my Fellowship at the Centre for Urban History. The urban history seminars and the specialist library have enabled me to rethink many of my assumptions. I have received assistance from many people who have been generous with their time and thoughts. In particular, I would like to thank Professor Richard Rodger whose knowledge of Scottish urban history has been invaluable. Bibliographical assistance supplied by Mark Livingston and Koen Bartels enabled greater understanding of sectarian and housing issues in Glasgow. Professor W.H. Fraser also provided guidance on matters of Scottish politics. Stephen Hopkins provided valuable bibliographical guidance on matters related to Northern Ireland and Belfast and Londonderry. Toby Lincoln provided vital critical appraisal that enabled me to clarify theoretical issues in respect of the problems of studying political corruption. The postgraduate students at the Centre for Urban History have been an inspiration for their sense of purpose and generosity, and I would like to thank Tom Hulme whose interest in civic traditions helped to inform my thinking and also Matthew Neale who helped to resolve technical issues concerning graphs and tables. Sir Peter Soulsby provided useful insights on the relations between council leaders and their parties. I would like to thank Professor Pat Thane for affording me the opportunity to present my thoughts about the Poulson case at the Contemporary British History Seminar at King's College London and Professor John Davis who encouraged me to present a paper about Glasgow's corruption at Glasgow University for the European Social Science History Conference in the spring of 2012. Special thanks must go to Professor Simon Gunn who had first encouraged me to research the matter of John Poulson's corruptions. His encouragement and gentle criticism have sustained me throughout the writing of the book. Lastly, I must thank my wife, Susan Brookes, who has lived with the research and writing over the last two years. Any shortcomings and errors are of course my own.

Peter Jones

Introduction

Base, bent, bribed, crooked, defiled, degenerate, depraved, dishonest, dissolute, fraudulent, rotten, shady, sleazy, tainted, unethical and venal. The lexicon of corruption draws us, potentially, into the linguistic undergrowth. It has been rarely visited by historians and would perhaps be better penetrated by criminologists. True, historians have made a place for the problem of political corruption but often only tangentially to illustrate part of a broader trend or to lace a narrative with some racy detail. To politicians, it is a political weapon to discredit opponents in the rough trade of power and advantage. To journalists, it is the bedfellow of scandal and is apparently essential to sell 'copy', especially for the popular newspapers. For the rest of society, it may seem remote and irrelevant. For political activists, it may reinforce assumptions about the political class. What then is corruption and why is it important for historians to study it? There are of course legal definitions but these are state specific. Britain is a highly regulated society, and so it is valuable to consider more theoretical definitions of political corruption developed by political scientists and cultural theorists. At the very least, corruption is the misuse of public office, by both elected representatives or by appointed officials, for personal gain or the gain of others who are connected to the office holders as family, clients, supporters or dependants.[1] It is a function of power exercised by those who can dispense benefits and advantages. In the sense of misuse of public office, political corruption is contrary to the social and cultural norms that prevail in a given society. Invariably, it involves a clandestine exchange between two markets – a political, bureaucratic market and a wider economic and social market – and it becomes manifest at the interface between public actors and private interests. The exchange in question – a bribe, favour or reward – represents, therefore, a transgression of public, legal and ethical norms rendering public decision-making unaccountable. However, precise definition and assessment of its importance remains difficult because of prevailing attitudes and beliefs about norms, values, public interests and standards of behaviour. Indeed, the social construction of reality is complexly formed and contested both socially and politically.[2] In this sense, then, perhaps corruption should be viewed as 'context dependent'[3] as Michel Foucault suggested because it is as much a social and political construction that can change over time as well as from one society or from one state to another. Corrupt exchanges are at the expense of the common good in favour of private, corporatist or client interests. In this sense, corruption is an abuse of power because it subverts approved mechanisms for the conduct of public affairs, and it enables private actors to secure preferential access to public resources such as contracts, finance, decision-making and information.[4] It involves a distortion of legal procedures creating a 'black market for resources over which politicians and bureaucrats have allocative power'.[5] When corrupt behaviour is especially widespread, it can permeate numerous, if not all, social relationships producing a low-trust society.[6]

There is dispute concerning the definitions of corruption because it can be both culturally contextualised and historically received through traditions and practices over time. For example, 'white' corruption is accepted by both political elites and by wider society. Corrupt individuals who become subject to the law often defend their actions by asserting that they did not do anything wrong on the grounds that 'everybody does it'. This was evident in the Poulson trials in the 1970s when Poulson claimed that gifts and hospitality were normal business practices. It was also apparent in the practice of 'personation' at elections in Belfast and justified by the adage 'vote early and vote often'. The so-called 'white' corruption has often been judged to be apparently acceptable in developing countries but also in Mediterranean societies such as Italy, Spain and Greece. It is justified as a means of getting things done and breaking bureaucratic gridlock. 'Black' corruption, however, is that which is practised by political elites but rejected by society at large and becomes apparent in corruption scandals which have frequently beset advanced political societies including the United States, France and Britain. Finally, there is also 'grey' corruption where societal perceptions of particular actions are ill-developed.[7] For example, the practice of business consultancies taken up by MPs or retired civil servants can constitute a conflict of interests between public position and private interests. Those that approve of such practices claim that such experience provides the public office holder with experience of the 'real' world outside the public domain. For those who are critical, it is argued that it confers the advantage of privileged information.

This preliminary review of definitions of corruption is not exhaustive, but it is sufficient to enable further questions to be asked which are particularly important for historians of British society. The pertinence of these questions can be highlighted further by some consideration of the effects of corruption, not least because it can have deleterious consequences for the conduct of politics and the well-being of society as a whole. It can result in the loss of tax revenues, a significant problem not just for developing countries but also for advanced states, such as Greece and Italy. This in turn may lead to the subversion of good governance because the state is unable to deliver basic requirements of statehood such as defence and law and order. Corruption often results in rising public expenditure because all transaction costs rise not just because of bribes and kickbacks but also because the costs of control via regulations and audit increase. Taxpayers may complain that they are not securing value for money from state services such as education and health. In extreme circumstances, markets may become 'rigged' to the detriment of all consumers, rich and poor alike. Further, corruption can retard political and economic development, which is reckoned to be a significant issue for Third World countries and in so-called failed states such as Somalia, Yemen and Afghanistan. But it is also a problem for advanced political societies including those of North America and Europe. Given such potentially serious consequences, it is important to seek explanations as to the causes of corruption.

Elites

Corruption exhibits certain distinct but interrelated characteristics, and it is important to consider some generalised causal factors. Corruption can often occur when powerful elites, particularly if they lack accountability, exert stability and control. In this traditional interpretation, elite power may be derived from patronage and clientism based on the 'vestiges of patrimonialism'.[8] The political elite within a given community may be disproportionately drawn from a single class, for example, the business class, resulting in a system of favours and benefits that are essentially corrupt. In a society or community[9] where the ruling elite is very powerful and the political opposition is weak or disorganised, corrupt behaviour can be rife as the elite fight for a share of the spoils. It may be that the ruling elite are so entrenched and unassailable that it comes to believe that the state's interests or the local government's interests and their own are conterminous. This type of cause is associated with oligarchy where the ruling group can perpetuate itself. It may involve processes of self-selection, patronage and clientage. Namier's classic account of England in the eighteenth century, *Politics in the Age of George III*, first published in 1928, demonstrates that MPs were in fact the placemen of aristocratic magnates such as the Duke of Newcastle. The baser motives and behaviours of the political class were notably venal so much so that politics was structured as a series of transactions based upon 'spoils and benefits'. Similar arrangements were also present in English local government in the eighteenth century where town corporations could be regarded as corrupt because they were self-perpetuating oligarchies such as Bristol, Ipswich, Leicester and Norwich.[10]

In local urban government in the twentieth century, it has been contended that corruption occurs where a local party fiefdom remains electorally unchallenged for long periods of time, thus creating a situation where the ruling party rides roughshod over all others and is unchallenged. It becomes a self-serving elite showing scant concern about matters of conduct or probity because accountability is weak. Where the ruling elite is extremely powerful and can monopolise office for long periods without being held to account and where the agents of the elite have considerable discretion, then the possibility of corruption is also great. This extension of elite theory has been referred to as 'principal–agent' theory and asserts that the agents of the ruling group or party will act according to the precepts of the political elite. In cities such as Glasgow and Belfast, principal–agent uniformity was achieved by means of patronage based on religion. In both cities, local council bureaucracies were recruited from Protestant communities, and so officials in housing departments in particular perpetuated social and economic advantages to their co-religionists. Elsewhere, local government in the north-east of England where the Labour Party has been dominant for long periods of time, there has been a particular version of elite control where council leaders – T. Dan Smith and Andrew Cunningham – became political 'bosses' not dissimilar to the 'city bosses' of American politics. It might also apply in the City of Westminster where Conservatives have enjoyed a monopoly of power: between 1964 and 2002, the Council was under uninterrupted control of the Conservative Party. In the 1980s, the leader of the council, Dame Shirley Porter, was able to subdue the council to her will with an almost ferocious zeal. Such a set of circumstances produces a situation where the ruling group becomes increasingly less accountable, and where the ruling group sets its own interests above those that they rule, then the likelihood of corruption becomes greater. Thus, Belfast was dominated by Protestant Unionists from 1929 until the onset of 'the troubles' in 1968. In Glasgow between 1945 and 1980, Labour was in a majority position for twenty-eight out of thirty-six years. In the thirty-two London Boroughs, Labour dominated from 1964 to 1994 controlling never less than twelve boroughs in 1982 and as many as twenty-one in 1974. All of these cities and boroughs experienced instances of corruption perpetrated by members of the ruling group and their respective administrations.

Modernisation

Elite theory can imply that corruption occurs primarily in stable or even static circumstances, but this is not always so as corruption also surfaces during periods of rapid change, modernisation or transition. The modernisation paradigm, Samuel Huntington suggested in 1968, may include industrialisation, urbanisation and upward social mobility. Modernisation creates new sources of wealth and power, and in politics, the entry of new groups with new forms of wealth who have not been accepted or assimilated into established power structures can produce accusations of corruption. This is because there are competing value systems or cultures. According to this argument, corruption occurs because of the 'absence of effective institutionalisation [during] an intense phase of modernisation'.[11] Further, modernisation involves the growth of state intervention to provide public goods and services – education, housing and health care, for example – together with an increase in state regulation inviting rule breaking. At the same time, the privatisation of state activity can also provide opportunity for sharp practice and corruption. The process of deindustrialisation and the transformation of society to a postmodern state can also generate social change with subsequent outbreaks of corruption. The modernisation thesis may have application to the corruptions of T. Dan Smith and John Poulson who exploited an intensive period of modernisation as the British state sought to expand the range of state goods and services in the form of building and construction programmes. The political dimension of modernisation has often been accompanied by a widening of political society via franchise extensions and the introduction of democracy. The consequent upward social mobility of new members into the political class who seek to make their way in the world and break the rules was recognised by de Tocqueville when he visited America in the early 1830s. He foresaw that an unintended consequence of the introduction of democracy was the growth of corruption[12] anticipating politicians who 'live by politics' rather than ideologues who 'live for politics'. The case of Glasgow in the 1930s provides a salient example: in 1933, Labour first gained control of Glasgow Corporation, which was certainly the outcome of the democratisation of local politics after 1918, but Labour's triumph was accompanied by corruption scandals. When corruption has become systemic in a particular society, it is important to recognise that politicians and political parties have a low propensity to tackle and eliminate corruption if exposed unless they can secure political change that is advantageous to themselves or their supporters. Invariably, the pressure to promote reform is slow to build despite, apparently, shocking revelations of corruption at particular moments. Often as not, corruption is exposed, in modern societies, by the press and other media for various motives – muckraking, sensationalism and reform. The press is often ahead of the police and the courts in the exposure of corruption. However, sensational press revelations often fail to translate into the introduction of reformed transparent political processes. A critical factor in this respect is the strength or weakness of civil society – clubs, societies, pressure groups, voluntary associations and so on – as it has been argued that civil society is a powerful resource that can keep politicians in check, especially if they resort to corruption. Conversely, if civil society is weak, then the potential for corruption is greater.[13]

State and civil society

There has been considerable scholarship in recent years on the issue of 'state building' and the creation of appropriate institutions to support the state. Francis Fukuyama has distilled much of this complex debate,[14] but the first issue to consider is the question of the legitimacy of the state as far as its people are concerned. At extreme levels, the legitimacy of the state is challenged in a time of revolution. However, lack of legitimacy can also give rise to corruption as politicians and members of society try to get round the bureaucracy of the state simply to survive and gain access to public goods and resources such as council housing and school places and access to travel visas and so on. In some respects, Belfast Corporation from 1931 until 1968 lacked legitimacy in the eyes of the Catholic minority, which constituted almost a quarter of the city's population. The Corporation was the local face of the Stormont government which represented the partition and the Treaty with Britain in 1921. Unrest and disorder might frequently paralyse the Belfast Corporation, and at times, the Stormont Parliament appointed commissioners to run the affairs of the city as the elected corporation was unable to do so. This problem of legitimacy spawned corrupt behaviour at all levels amongst politicians, the police and the people of Belfast who sought to get round the *immobilisme* of Belfast's local government. The question of state legitimacy has also raised interest in more recent times to the question of 'state building'. Weak states are seen as vulnerable to corruption. Predatory elites may plunder the resources of the state in rapacious fashion. For the state builders then, the supply of institutions – parliaments, judiciaries, municipalities and so on – can act as critical counterweights to the threat of corruption.[15] However, it overlooks the fact that the prevailing mode of conduct of politics is a manifestation of the uneven distribution of power and corrupt actions can be perpetrated by both the powerful and the less powerful. They may take different forms reflecting the asymmetry of the relations between the participants. Institutions may be able to regulate such actions, but very often they cannot address the realities of the distribution of power.[16] Nevertheless, for many theorists, a strong civil society is a crucial condition of a strong democracy. In essence, 'civil society has an institutional core constituted by voluntary associations outside the sphere of the state and the economy'.[17] At local level, urban government is often mediated through a range of competing institutions and practices which can make for maladministration if not corruption.[18] They can act as checks on an overbearing state challenging its actions and holding it to account. Further, these groups have a powerful capacity to socialise individuals to the cultural life of a society shaping ethical standards and promoting 'reciprocity, moral obligation, duty toward community, and trust'.[19] However, such organisations may not be able to do anything about those who are corrupt or who seek to break the law. Scepticism of this view has a long pedigree. Thus, Machiavelli asserted that men are 'ungrateful, fickle, liars and deceivers ... [and] ... they are wicked and that they will always give vent to their malignity that is in their minds when opportunity offers'.[20] More recently, Robert Putnam has challenged the institution-building thesis of its advocates suggesting that 'designers of new institutions are often writing on water [and] that institutional reforms alter behaviour is a hypothesis not an axiom'. Nevertheless, it is certainly likely to be the case that where civil society is weak, the possibility of corruption is great, and perhaps the most notable example of this is the Italian state since 1945.[21]

Markets

Economists have been adept at demonstrating the relationships between markets and corrupt behaviour. In essence, corruption occurs in situations where there are scarce resources. Thus, where the state intervenes to control the market as in a rationing system in wartime, for example, there will be an inducement to break the rules and regulations to access scarce resources. Those that do may be seen as traitors and unpatriotic. In the British case, the existing legislation against corruption was strengthened in the First World War, and stiffer penalties were introduced for those found guilty of bribery or breaking rationing regulations. For economists, then, there is a direct relationship between imperfect or regulated markets and corrupt behaviour. The logic of this approach implies that free markets are the best deterrent against corrupt behaviour. This is an especially pertinent issue in the field of development economics where Third World countries are the recipients of economic aid and charity. Funds do not always flow directly to the point of need and are often tapped as they pass through the hands of politicians and officials. International banking and development institutions including the IMF, the World Bank and the OECD have been keen to advocate free trade, free markets and small states for such situations. The donor–recipient conduit of economic aid has special relevance to Britain because of regional policies which began to emerge in the wake of the Great Depression after 1929. The designation of special areas – Clydeside and the west of Scotland, South Wales and north-east England – meant that they became regions in need. The conduit that delivered those funds could be tapped at many points: by civil servants, by local politicians and officers and by builders and developers who often believed that they were worthy of some additional reward. This would seem to have been the case with T. Dan Smith who became chairman of the Northern Economic Development Council in 1965. More generally, economists have argued that corruption opportunities can often be located at points of marginal utility which is dependent on the average price of public goods and services compared with those in the free market. This became a critical issue for local governments in the wake of public subsidy for housing. In the 1930s, getting a council house which was provided at a subsidised rent was a highly attractive proposition. However, the supply of council houses was inelastic, and this meant that the politics of council housebuilding and allocation to tenants was especially competitive, leading to bribery and pressure. Many councils developed priority criteria as a means of allocating a house to those in need. If local housing officials had discretionary power, it often made them vulnerable to bribery. They might not have been the instigators, but the opportunities for collusion between housing officers and would-be tenants were legion. There were certainly some extremely elaborate schemes in Glasgow, Belfast and elsewhere. These cases perhaps act as grist to the mill of the free market economists who are keen to link the issue of corruption to the issue of state size. For them, an oversized state is potentially always vulnerable to corruption. Their view is that the allocation of resources is best left to the market.[22] Even here though, it is not straightforward as the transition from one type of economic system or market arrangement to another might generate corrupt opportunities. Thus, where states have sold public assets on the free market, the opportunity for sharp dealing and chicanery has always been a risk as shown in Britain in the 1980s with the right-to-buy scheme of council houses. There was no more flagrant example of corrupt behaviour than that of Dame Shirley Porter in her manipulation of the sale of council flats in the City of Westminster in what amounted to gerrymandering electoral wards. It illustrates that economic theory and political motives cannot always be easily separated.

Sociology

Sociologists have made important contributions to our understanding of the causes and the nature of corruption.[23] Perhaps one of the most obvious issues in relation to corruption in this context is the notion of acceptance. The stoic refrain that all politicians and officials are corrupt supplemented with a 'that's how it is' view of the world creates an environment in which the corrupt can prosper. In part, this may stem from attitudes of deference and respect that other parts of society show towards politicians and public officials. It may be difficult to recall a time when politicians were respected and held in public esteem. Rapid social change often creates new social types – parvenus, yuppies and nouveaux riches – who possess new types of wealth and exhibit new types of behaviours that can be seen as potentially corrupt. Indeed, these new social types may believe that it is legitimate to resort to any tactics to get on and be successful. In this sense, this manifestation of corrupt behaviour may represent a failed assimilation of those new groups into what has been called respectable society. Further, depending on the degree of social stratification and the extent to which upward social mobility is easy or difficult in any particular society, the movement from one class to another involves learning new codes of behaviour in order to gain acceptance. Failure to secure acceptance may result in attempts to buy-in. This would certainly have been the case with John Poulson. His craving for recognition and honours led him to throw money around and gain favour.

Sociologists have also provided insights into the values and attitudes of particular subgroups or even subcultures. This is a useful stance in relation to the study of corruption since those who are involved in corrupt transactions – businessmen and politicians – may see their behaviour as normal because they live and work in a closed world that creates its own 'situational morality' with its own norms and values.[24] When the corrupt are arrested and prosecuted, their defence is often that 'everyone does it'. The process of law faces those accused with a challenge to their privately normal behaviour. Other defences might include there 'was no harm done' or that the result – a new housing scheme, town centre redevelopment or school – was of benefit to society. Moreover, the politicians who found themselves subject to the law would argue that they had only a modest recompense for their voluntary effort. For them, public service and private gain were not incompatible. In British society in the 1960s and 1970s, the existence of such views was not uncommon, but their articulation created a challenge to the prescribed boundaries of public life. This clash is at the centre of the analysis of corruption and particularly in British society which has assumed order and acceptance of public rules.

Culture

Perhaps one of the most interesting developments in historiography has been the development of cultural history.[25] The application of a cultural dimension to an examination of corruption is potentially powerful. Within the compass of culture, it would be valuable to consider the nature of the ethical environment of any given society. Further, what are the factors that shape the ethical environment? The nature of the ethical environment will also enable us to understand important elements of social capital such as trust and the strength or weakness of civil society. The ethical environment of any society shapes what is regarded as right or wrong, acceptable and unacceptable. It also shapes individual and group identity. This is crucial in matters of campaigns against and exposure of corruption. These considerations are often vital when examining the exposure of corruption. We will see this with the Independent Labour Party (ILP) campaign led by John McGovern and William Leonard in Glasgow in the 1930s to expose the culture of graft within the Labour Party. It has also been apparent in the culture of the Fourth Estate, namely, that the press has a duty to investigate and publish in the public interest. The ethical environment then shapes prevailing morality and sets standards of behaviour and conduct, and this was evident in Nolan's first report which sought to restate public morality in respect of those who held public office. Perhaps Nolan's Seven Principles of Public Life – selflessness, integrity, objectivity, accountability, openness, honesty and leadership – were an attempt to recover older virtues of self-control and to draw attention to the idea of good character as the basis of moral behaviour in public life? The ethical environment is itself shaped by religion and other codes of life and conduct. It may include a sense of public duty that is coupled intrinsically with codes of behaviour that entail honour, decency, selflessness, integrity and probity.[26] In this argument, if the ethical environment places high premium on decency, probity and integrity, then it should follow that the incidence of corruption would be low and that when corrupt behaviour appears, then it is challenged. Conversely, if the ethical environment does not value honesty and integrity but rather is shaped by an urge for status acquisition and wealth, then it might be that the incidence of corruption is high. Such grand unifying theory should, however, be treated cautiously although the nature of shift in the ethical environment, in Britain, for example, from 1940 to the 1960s, may shed light on some instances of corrupt behaviour.

The ethical environment can also determine the degree of trust that prevails in any society.[27] In this respect, trust is a barometer that can indicate whether we might witness corrupt behaviour or conversely honesty and fair dealing. The centrality of trust for stable political relations and a functioning society had been identified by John Locke at the end of the seventeenth century, but it has taken on new significance because of growing concern about the growth of corruption. According to this argument, high-trust societies have low transaction costs and can therefore achieve social co-operation, order and stability with minimal state intervention. However, in low-trust societies, governments are required to legislate and regulate, and this results in increased transactional costs. This would seem to be the case in Italy but also in Belfast in Northern Ireland.[28] In the British case, we might think of it as a high-trust society although there are pockets and areas where there is low trust and government has sought to regulate in areas such as planning or alternatively to follow a policy of laissez faire particularly in relation to the conduct of MPs. Trust is critical for the growth of an effective civil society with strong voluntary organisations and individuals prepared to commit to the public domain. Civil society flourishes where there is a 'proclivity for community'.[29] In these circumstances, trust flourishes because there has been a successful 'habituation to the moral norms of the community [as well as the promotion of] the acquisition of virtues like loyalty, honesty and dependability'. The 'proclivity for community'[30] and its attendant virtues constitute social capital which in turn creates social cohesiveness and political order. However, although 'social capital is the crucible of trust', it is not evenly distributed throughout society because group formation or community is consequent upon the generation of shared values and therefore an 'organic solidarity'.[31] Where organic solidarity is not present or indeed rights-based individualism prevails, then there is a breakdown of shared values and the organisations associated with those shared values wither away leaving potential corruption unchallenged and simply accepted.

Conclusion

As will already be apparent, corruption is a slippery term, but an acceptance of the hypothesis that corruption is 'context dependent' which cannot exclusively be examined entirely via state laws is an important feature of the subsequent analysis. That societal apprehension of corrupt behaviour is based upon an aggregation of numerous subjectivities should not be overlooked and it is important to recognise that social tolerance or intolerance of corruption is often the starting point for reform campaigns. The laws and regulations that follow or fail to gain political traction have special relevance to the British case. Indeed, for those who are involved in corruption, their individual transactions with other members of the corruption network may well be regarded as normal and reasonable.[32] Appreciation of the theoretical models of social scientists and cultural theorists may provide some explanatory underpinning, but historical analysis also demonstrates the uniqueness of particular corrupt moments. All theoretical models have their limitations, and in the narrative that follows, it will become apparent that different theories of the state and corruption can coexist at micro level.

Chapter 1 will examine the matter of perception and awareness of the problem of corruption and how reform has been slow to develop. Chapter 2 deals with the role of the civic tradition and how civil society has been an important although diminishing inhibitor of corrupt behaviour in British urban society. Chapter 3 will examine corruption in Glasgow as a classic case that the growth of democracy can produce the unintended outcome of corruption. Chapter 4 examines the important corruptions of John Poulson and T. Dan Smith and considers their emblematic status. Chapter 5 scrutinises the role of Dame Shirley Porter in the politics of the City of Westminster. The conclusion draws these matters together and considers the structures of corrupt environments and the origins of the corrupters themselves.

Notes

1 Della Porta, D. and A. Vanucci, *Hidden Order of Corruption: An Institutional Approach* (Farnham: Ashgate, 2012); Lambsdorff, J., *The Institutional Economics of Corruption* (Cambridge: Cambridge University Press, 2007).

2 Berger, P. and T. Luckmann, *The Social Construction of Reality* (London: Penguin, 1984).

3 Flyvbjerg, B., 'Habermas and Foucault: thinkers for civil society', *British Journal of Sociology*, 49: 2 (1998), pp. 210–33; Luxon, N. 'Ethics and subjectivity', *Political Theory*, 36: 3 (2008), pp. 377–402.

4 Della Porta, D. and Y. Meny (eds.), *Democracy and Corruption in Europe* (London: Pinter, 1997), p. 4.

5 Della Porta and Vanucci, *Hidden Order*, pp. 6–7.

6 Fukuyama, F., *Trust: The Social Virtues of Prosperity* (New Haven: Free Press, 1995), p. 358.

7 Heidenheimer, A., *Political Corruption: Readings in Comparative Analysis* (New York: Holt Rinehart and Winston, 1970), pp. 54–5.
8 Della Porta and Meny, *Democracy and Corruption*, p. 175.
9 Hunter, F., *Community Power Structure* (Chapel Hill: University of North Carolina Press, 1953).
10 Sweet, R., *The English Town, 1680–1840* (Harlow: Longman, 1999), pp. 104–5.
11 Huntington, S., *Political Order: Readings in Comparative Analysis* (New Haven: Yale University Press, 1968), pp. 59–71.
12 Tocqueville, A., de, *Democracy in America* (New York: Alfred Knopf, 1994), pp. 225–7.
13 Banfield, E., *The Moral Basis of a Backward Society* (New York: Free Press, 1958), pp. 83–101; Ginsborg, P., *Italy and Its Discontents 1980–2001*: Family, Civil Society and the State (London: Penguin, 2001); Putnam, R., Leonardi and Y.N. Rafaella, *Making Democracy Work: Civic Traditions in Modern Italy* (Princeton: Princeton University Press, 1994).
14 Fukuyama, F., *State Building: Governance and World Order in the Twenty First Century* (London: Profile Books, 2005); and *Origins of Political Order: From Pre-human Times to the French Revolution* (London: Profile Books, 2011).
15 Fukuyama, *State Building*, pp. 60–9.
16 Machiavelli, N., *The Discourses of Niccolo Machiavelli* (London: Routledge Kegan Paul, 1970); Rousseau, J.J., *On the Social Contract* (London: Penguin, 2004); Gramsci, A., *Selections from the Prison Notebooks* (London: Lawrence and Wishart, 1971); Lukes, S., *Power: A Radical View* (London: Palgrave, 2004).
17 Flyvbjerg, 'Habermas and Foucault', pp. 210–33.
18 Moore, J. and J. Smith (eds.), *Corruption in Urban Politics and Society, Britain 1780–1950* (Aldershot: Ashgate, 2007); and Morris, R.J. and R.H. Trainor (eds.), *Urban Governance: Britain and Beyond Since 1750* (Aldershot: Ashgate, 2000).
19 Fukuyama, *Trust*.
20 Machiavelli, *Discourses*.
21 Putnam et al., *Making Democracy Work*.
22 There is an extensive literature on this subject which can be found on the websites of the OECD, the World Bank and the IMF. A preliminary bibliography can also be found in Goudie A. and D. Stasavage, 'Corruption: the issues', *Working Paper No. 122, OECD Development Centre* (1997), pp. 1–53.
23 Chibnall, S. and P. Saunders, 'Worlds apart: notes on the social reality of corruption', *British Journal of Sociology*, 28 (1977), pp. 138–54; Flyvbjerg, 'Habermas and Foucault', pp. 210–33.
24 Chibnall and Saunders, 'Worlds apart', pp. 138–52.
25 For introductions see Gunn, S., *History and Cultural Theory* (Harlow: Longman, 2006); and Burke, P., *What Is Cultural History* (Cambridge: Polity Press, 2008).
26 Grayling, A., *Ideas That Matter: A Personal Guide for the Twenty First Century* (London: Phoenix, 2009), pp. 179–85.
27 Fukuyama, *Trust*; Locke, J., *Two Treatises of Government* (Cambridge: Cambridge University Press, 1967).
28 Foster, R., *Modern Ireland 1600–1972* (London: Allen Lane, 1988).
29 Fukuyama, *Trust*, p. 10.
30 *Ibid.*, p. 26–7.
31 Durkheim, E., *Division of Labour* (London: Macmillan, 1984).
32 Nuijten, M. and G. Anders, *Corruption and the Secret of the Law: A Legal Anthropological Perspective* (Aldershot: Ashgate, 2007), pp. 1–24.

1 Perceptions and anxieties

> There is widespread current disquiet about conduct in local government, following recent prosecutions for corruption. Any general judgement on the honesty of local authorities is necessarily to a great extent subjective.
>
> Lord Redcliffe-Maud (1974)[1]

In his evidence to the Nolan Commission which had been set up in October 1994, Lord Blake suggested that the problem of scandal emanating from malpractice, corruption and misconduct in British politics went in cycles. The period 1865–95 had been trouble free, but from 1895 to 1930 there had been a lot. He cited in particular the activities of Lloyd George, Chancellor of the Exchequer, and Rufus Isaacs, Attorney General, in 1912, both of whom had speculated in Marconi shares with, apparently, the benefit of insider information. It was a great scandal and the press had a field day. It did not though significantly damage the government or in particular Lloyd George whose career continued to soar. By way of contrast, Blake opined that the more recent scandals – 'cash for questions' and general revelations of 'sleaze' – which had been instrumental in the establishment of Lord Nolan's Commission paled 'into insignificance compared with the Marconi scandal'.[2] Marconi was the first of a series of landmark cases which was to shape the landscape of corruption in the early twentieth century. The other cases that related to national government involved munitions contracts in 1921 which occasioned the establishment of the Tribunal system of inquiry; the sale of honours in 1922, again involving Lloyd George, for party funds; currency speculation involving civil servants in 1928; and the Belcher case in 1948.[3] Blake's assessment was perhaps intuitive and, as he admitted to his inquisitors, based on his reading of Geoffrey Searle's study of corruption in Britain between 1895 and 1930.[4] Does Blake's assessment suffice?

At first sight, there is much to commend his rather pragmatic view. Between 1929 and 1948 there were three major cases: Glasgow in 1933, Newcastle in 1944 and the case of John Belcher, a Board of Trade Minister, in 1948. After the

Belcher case, there was little on the horizon to cause alarm until the trials of John Poulson, the Yorkshire architect, in the early 1970s. Following the Poulson scandal, there then appeared a further hiatus until the revelations of gerrymandering by the leader of Westminster City Council, Dame Shirley Porter, arising from the report of the District Auditor in January 1994.[5] In some respects, the Porter case was overshadowed by the 'cash for questions' scandal when *The Guardian* reported that Mohamed Al-Fayed, the proprietor of Harrods' department store, had via the lobby firm, Greer Associates, paid two MPs – Neil Hamilton and Tim Smith – to ask questions on his behalf in the House of Commons.[6] These scandals were notable for the subsequent furore, but they obscured the fact that not all corrupt activity becomes a scandal of national proportions. Indeed, much corrupt activity remains hidden and may remain undetected. Thus, Blake's claim concerning the cyclical nature of corruption may not be measuring the contours of corruption but rather fluctuations in the revelations of corruption that became scandalous causing the perception of corruption to impact upon the public imagination. In order to move beyond Lord Blake's provisional assessment, some attempt at measurement of the occurrence and frequency of corruption crises should be undertaken. Subsequently, it becomes possible to examine how apprehension of corruption was linked or not to the articulation of a reform critique by political activists.

Definitions and measurements

The problem of corruption has been far greater than an examination of cases that became national scandals alone reveals. Whether British public life has become more corrupt may not ultimately be settled, but it will be shown that British attempts to confront and find solutions for corruption have been deflected by assumptions informed by late Victorian liberalism and by British imperial and civic traditions. The account and analysis that ensues will concentrate on local urban government, primarily. However, it will also be necessary to comment on developments and themes in national politics. The critique of corruption as articulated by those who were concerned about it evolved gradually over the sixty-five years under review. At the beginning of the period, corruption in local government was centred on drink licences, council contracts, provision of council housing, council services and facilities such as markets, council employment and elections. Later, it arose in relation to planning and redevelopment, the misuse of information and the failure on the part of local councillors to declare their interests in council contracts. The most important area though was that related to planning and urban development, which was an activity where national and local government procedures converged. Further, as cities changed their functions, particularly in the wake of the process of deindustrialisation, so their relationships with central government were also redefined. Moreover, as patterns of governance changed, so the sources of corruption altered. For example, the Glasgow application for European City of Culture in 1990 plunged the city into yet another corruption scandal resulting in the suspension of Pat Lally, the Lord Provost.

The contention that corruption occurred in cycles conceals the fact that there has been an undercurrent of corruption located in many places. That does not mean that such a judgement is unimportant. In the first instance, popular perceptions of the extent of corruption have perhaps been derived from press reports. In the earlier part of the twentieth century, corruption was seen to be more prevalent overseas than in Britain. It was not until the early 1960s that press reports of domestic corruption outweighed the report of overseas cases. Then in the later 1960s and 1970s, corruption cases reported in *The Times* and *The Guardian* increased dramatically, and this increase coincided with the corruption trials of John Poulson, T. Dan Smith and numerous others (see Appendix). Thereafter, reportage declined before it rose again in the 1990s coinciding with the Nolan Commission (1994) and the general allegations of 'sleaze' widespread in the run-up to the 1997 election. At the same time, international reports on corruption also rose dramatically as the 'clean hands' operation progressed in Italy after February 1992, and in France, the cases against Maurice Arreckx, the Mayor of Toulon, along with the scandal involving Michel Noir, Mayor of Lyon, also hit the headlines.[7]

Newspaper reports present problems: bias and the political preferences of the proprietors and editors, sensationalism and confusion between corruption and its journalistic companion, scandal. Such objections imply caution, but perception of corrupt behaviour cannot be dismissed. The matter might be settled by plotting the actual number of prosecutions for corruption, provided that some account for under-recording and undetected crime could be factored-in to the calculations. The broad contours of prosecuted defendants for corruption offences against the Public Bodies Corrupt Practices Acts (1889, 1906 and 1916) reveal that prosecutions remained at a low level throughout the period 1890 to 1970 with two minor surges around 1916–20 and 1930–35. The corruption laws established the narrowest definition of corruption in that they applied to employees and elected councillors and other representatives of public bodies making it illegal for them to use their public positions, elected or employed, for personal advantage. Thus, bribing public officials was illegal from 1889. Councillors who had procured bribes, rewards and gifts or used their public position to secure the advantage of their relatives, friends or clients could also be subject to prosecution. The prosecutions under these acts show similar fluctuations to the incidence of newspaper reports suggesting a similarity between perception and awareness of corruption on the one hand and actual prosecutions for offences under the acts on the other. The broad patterns are readily apparent: the initial measure in 1889 probably had little impact, and it was not until after 1906 when the scope of the law was widened to capture agents that the rate of prosecutions began to rise. The increase in 1916–20 was a function of increased state regulation to fight the War and a decrease in public toleration of wrongdoing. In this sense, so-called 'grey' corruption had become 'black'. In the period 1930 to 1935, the increase was probably a reflection of economic conditions as increasing numbers of the urban populations were involved in various bureaucratic transactions with their local governments for housing, poor relief and even employment. This appears to fit the classic modernisation thesis that corruption increases when the role of the state expands.

For the whole of the period 1895 to 1990, the average prosecution rate was around twenty-four per year, but the overall trend from 1971 to 1980 was steeply upward. In fact, three-quarters of all prosecutions, over 1730 cases, occurred in the twenty years between 1971 and 1990 indicating a prosecution rate of 87 cases per year, and more than half of all prosecutions occurred between 1971 and 1980 generating a prosecution rate of 120 per year. The remaining 575 prosecutions were spread across the first eighty years of the period indicating a prosecution rate of around only seven cases a year. Apparently then, Britain had become, by this measure, more corrupt over the period. However, changes in Home Office collection, recording and presenting reports to parliament changed over the period (see Appendix). Nevertheless, the peaks coincide with major cases – munitions in 1920–21, Glasgow in 1933, Poulson and T. Dan Smith in 1974–75 and Shirley Porter in the late 1980s and early 1990s. There is a remarkable synchronicity between the perception of corruption as indicated by newspaper reportage and the actual prosecution rate.

Before confidence can be established with the generalisation that British political culture had become more corrupt, an examination of trends over the longer run from the late eighteenth century down to 1990–95 will broaden the context. This is important because the major investigations of the 1970s – conducted by Lords Redcliffe-Maud and Salmon – avoided the matter of discerning long-term trends. Redcliffe-Maud recorded cases from 1964 to 1969, and Lord Salmon's Commission recorded cases from 1964 to 1972. This was information readily to hand, and they found that the number of cases prosecuted under the Corruption Acts between 1964 and 1972 was no more than four a year, and if discipline under the Local Government Acts involving a failure by councillors to declare their interests are taken into account, then there were eight or nine cases a year. Lord Salmon's Commission though does give a very good picture of the types and sources of corrupt behaviour as well as the occupations of those who were prosecuted. Of the 200 people prosecuted between 1964 and 1972, almost half were local authority officers, and more than fifteen per cent were elected councillors, aldermen and mayors. Thus, local authority employees and local politicians made up sixty-five per cent of all the accused. This observation was qualified by Lord Salmon who was at pains to record the facts that there were 26,000 elected local councillors in the United Kingdom and seven million local authority employees, suggesting that the number of prosecutions was therefore a very small proportion of the numbers of people involved in local authority activity. He did not however grapple with the issue that not all of that population had the opportunity to be involved in corrupt transactions. Nor did he deal with the problem that the number of prosecutions was a smaller proportion of the number of potential cases notified to the police. In fact, between 1964 and 1978, almost a third of cases did not proceed to trial.[8] Many investigations were abandoned because of the problem of proving corrupt intent. In addition to local authorities, the other major sources of corruption were to be found in the nationalised industries: cases that involved employees in British Railways, the National Coal Board and gas, electricity and water authorities made up more than sixteen per cent of all the cases. The rest were to be found amongst prison officers, driving test examiners, immigration officers and civil servants. At the same time, we should consider that corruption involves a transaction between two or more people. Typically particular areas of activity were especially vulnerable. These included inspection activities by clerks of works and water authority inspectors, rating and valuation, and attempts to bribe inspectors to approve or turn a blind eye made up almost a fifth of all cases. Planning, housing tenancy, local authority contracts, market stalls and the issuing of drink licences made up more than a third of all cases, and councillors who failed to declare their interest when speaking and voting in the council chamber made up another third of all cases. The failure to declare an interest was not a contravention of the Corruption Acts, but it was contrary to the regulations consolidated into the Local Government Act 1933. Failure to declare was not an indictable offence although it was a matter of disciplinary sanction by a local authority.

The inherent limitations of prosecution information, which included changes in patterns of record as well as under-recording and, therefore, prosecution rates, suggest some alternative methods of measurement. An examination of the longer-term trend using a perception measure rather than a prosecution rate reveals that the overall trend from the late eighteenth century to the early twenty-first century was downwards (see Appendix). Admittedly, there were some dramatic fluctuations often coinciding with reform campaigns where the 'cry' of corruption was used by reformers as an argument to open up the political system. There was a considerable disparity between different places suggesting the perception of corruption varied according to both time and place. Sensitivity to corruption would seem to have been most marked in Bristol, then Leeds and then Glasgow. Indeed, newspaper reportage in the local provincial press would seem to have been greater than reportage in the national press. From the late eighteenth century through to the twenty-first century, using national and provincial newspapers, there was a remarkably diverse picture. Admittedly, the national picture is clear with corruption peaking in the late eighteenth century, declining and then rising around 1830, peaking again in mid-century up to the 1870s and tailing away in the twentieth century. Overall, the trend is downwards, and the peaks coincide with the contours of the political reform process – the franchise extension in 1832, secret ballot in 1872, party funding and Marconi in 1906–12, Poulson in the 1970s and MPs expenses at the beginning of the twenty-first century. In provincial centres, there were other patterns. In the nineteenth century, Bristol and Leeds were hotspots within the reform movement suggesting heightened levels of interest in those cities, and in Glasgow there appears to be a residual persistence of corruption, much of it apparently low level. Whatever these measures tell us, it certainly dispels the claim that corruption was not a problem in British local politics but rather that it has had a low-level presence for a long period.

There is no easy way to measure the levels of corruption that have existed in British society in the recent past. Lord Redcliffe-Maud's dictum that apprehension of corruption is indeed subjective[9] would seem to have much credence. At the beginning of the period, perceptions of corruption by political and social elites were punctuated by assertions of broken trust, lost pride and the incipient breakdown of civic institutions. Newspaper reportage does provide a vital insight, and the comparison between national and local perceptions only underscores the difficulties of measurement of the phenomenon. It was not surprising then that reform critiques were slow to gestate as it was not until the 1970s that a more determined effort to reform local government emerged.

A final measure to consider in relation to the perception of corruption is that of the opinion poll. George Gallup had developed public opinion polling in the United States in the 1930s originally to discover voting intention, and in 1936 he successfully reported that Franklin Roosevelt would win the presidential election. It was not just the predictive quality of polling that was apparently attractive as it became increasingly wide ranging and sophisticated in its techniques. In 1973, an *Opinion Research Centre* poll conducted on behalf of *The Times* revealed that forty per cent of respondents thought that local councillors were able to obtain a dishonest financial advantage from being on the council. A similar body of opinion was in favour of taking major building contracts away from local councils. The revelations concerning John Poulson were beginning to percolate into the public domain, and these no doubt influenced public opinion. Further, younger people were more suspicious of councillors' motives than older respondents. Later research conducted for the Nolan Commission in the early 1990s suggested that politicians – ministers, MPs and local councillors – were generally regarded as untrustworthy along with journalists, estate agents and senior managers within the Health Service. By contrast, family doctors, head teachers, judges and policemen were perceived to be trustworthy. The esteem in which politicians were held would also seem to have declined, according to a Gallup Poll conducted in 1995, which found that the public thought that MPs told lies and sought public office for their own personal gain. Such perceptions may provide a proxy measure of the prevalence or otherwise of corrupt behaviour. These sorts of perceptions were to be found elsewhere in

Europe. For example, in France, a Sofres Poll conducted in 1990 indicated that fifty-five per cent of French people thought their politicians were corrupt.[10] In Italy, there were on average over 500 cases of corruption per year between 1963 and 1975, and by 1979–86 this had risen to an average of over 800 cases per year.[11] Comparisons with other countries are, however, difficult to interpret although such a task has been undertaken by the *Transparency International* organisation, which produces an annual Corruption Perception Index, which has ranked the United Kingdom seventeenth in 2009. Countries perceived as less corrupt than the United Kingdom included New Zealand, Canada, Singapore and the Nordic countries. Countries perceived to be more corrupt included the United States, France and Italy. Whatever the scientific claims of such research might suggest, perhaps Richard Hoggart's intuitive gleanings of working-class male opinion in the 1960s England of politicians revealed as much as the scientific survey. Of those he interviewed, the general opinion was negative. Politicians were 'twisters and crooks', 'out for their own ends', 'feathering their own nests' and 'looking after number one'.[12] So although there can be no certainty, there are at least three broad measures of the cyclical pattern of corruption. The incidence of newspaper articles in broadsheet national newspapers, *The Times* and *The Guardian*, suggests that awareness of corruption and its potential seriousness shifted markedly in the 1970s with articles about corruption in Britain rising sharply between 1966 and 1977 exceeding, for the first time in the twentieth century, reportage of corruption overseas. Secondly, the prosecution rate of corruption had hovered at a low level for most of the twentieth century rising sharply after 1966 up to 1980 before declining in the early 1980s and then rising again after 1985, suggesting a new baseline that was higher than that which had prevailed for the earlier part of the century. Thirdly, the perception of corruption over the long run from the late eighteenth century to the early twentieth century suggests a long-run decline in the overall perception of the extent of corruption suggesting that the period 1790–1830 was more corrupt than the later twentieth century.

The legacy of eighteenth century corruption has often been the reference point for politicians in the twentieth century who claim that contemporary problems were less than those apparently prevalent in the eighteenth century. This is in line with prevailing interpretations: 'Corruption was the single most important political issue of the eighteenth century. It never lost its importance, yet there was never much danger of a root and branch approach to eliminating it'.[13] Corruption then was seemingly brought under control as government became more representative and as the state became increasingly efficient over a period from *c.*1830 to *c.*1890. This has been attributed to the challenge of international competition with Britain and Prussia/Germany perhaps becoming the most efficient and least corrupt of the European states.[14] However, the later twentieth century witnessed a reassertion of the problem of corruption with much of it located in local government which had become a service provider for the delivery of the state's social goods – housing, health and education. Such an interpretation, however, is not clouded by current concerns of corrupt behaviour within Britain's new political class that emerged from the later 1980s and into the twenty-first century.[15] Given the shifting forms of contemporary concern about corruption, it was not remarkable that the development of a reform critique was slow to evolve.

Reform critique and discourses

Overall, the period 1929 to 1994, from the Local Government Act to the setting up of the Nolan Commission on Standards in Public Life, can be divided into three phases: the first from 1929 to 1948, the second from 1949 to 1974 and the last from 1975 to 1994. In the first phase, the debate about the problem of corruption was conducted against a background of a well-regulated electoral system since corruption in parliamentary and local elections had largely been eliminated by the series of reforms to widen the franchise between 1832 and 1928[16] and legislation to control behaviour at elections by means of secret ballot in 1872 and limits on election expenses in 1883. The exception to this was, of course, Northern Ireland, after the Treaty of 1921, where the electoral system increasingly lacked legitimacy in the eyes of the Catholic minority. Further, between 1889 and 1916, the three pieces of legislation, the Public Bodies Corrupt Practices Acts, were designed to control the conduct of public office holders and public officials suggesting a specific definition of their duties: they were not expected to use their public office for enrichment. Thus, on the face of it, Britain was a well-regulated political society and not regarded as corrupt. However, there were dark corners where the system worked less well. Additionally, there were few instances of electoral corruption in English and Welsh constituencies, and there were only seventeen instances of electoral petitions in respect of parliamentary elections between 1900 and 1961 where the courts decided that the election result could not stand. A quarter of the cases in question had been in Ireland prior to the establishment of the Free State in 1921. Additionally, there were numerous examples of electoral corruption in Scotland and Northern Ireland after 1929, principally in Glasgow, Belfast and Londonderry where the practice of personation was considerable.[17]

The development of a reform discourse about corruption began to emerge after 1918 when revelations of corruption in the Ministry of Munitions prompted Captain Charles Loseby, Conservative MP for Bradford East and a supporter of Lloyd George's coalition government, to raise the matter in the House of Commons. Loseby claimed he had compelling evidence that a civil servant had ordered members of his department to destroy documents lest they were scrutinised by the Treasury's auditors. Loseby's request was couched in traditional language for the time: he was anxious to secure the 'purity of administration' within a government department. The legislation was rushed through Parliament resulting in the Tribunals of Inquiry (Evidence) Act 1921. This was an important development since the Government was under considerable pressure to settle the accounts of numerous contractors. There were still almost 58,000 accounts unsettled, and the need to expedite this problem quickly was also highlighted by the case of a Sheffield tungsten manufacturer – Murex Limited – which announced its intention to take legal action, because of an unpaid account, against the Ministry of Munitions.[18]

The Tribunals Act then established a remarkable device enabling the state to investigate any matter of public concern by means of a Tribunal chaired by a senior law officer. The problem of outstanding payments had prompted the Ministry to set up an Accounts Liquidation Committee which had discretionary powers to settle the payments, and these accounts were examined by civil servants known as Ledger Investigators. Problems in the Ministry had surfaced at the end of hostilities, and the press had mounted numerous assaults on the Ministry deriding it as 'moribund'.[19] There had also been an instance of petty corruption where a junior civil servant had fraudulently been involved in the disposal of Rolls-Royce aircraft engines.[20] As the post-war slump began to deepen and pressures for public spending cuts began to mount, the press shifted its fire to contractors – shell and armament manufacturers – who owed the Ministry sums amounting to £12 million. It was against this background that Charles Loseby made his claim that there was extensive irregularity and even corruption and that there were 'vast accounts paid without investigation' in the hurried winding-up of the Ministry.[21] His accusations were dependent on information received from the Ledger Investigators who had reported that a principal civil servant, Ernest Sutton, at a meeting in October or November 1920, had told them to destroy documents and working papers or indeed lose them because 'the Exchequer and Audit Department were nosing round into the accounts' and that it was 'essential that we cover-up our traces'.[22] Loseby claimed that Sutton's casual candour emanated from a belief that he was protected by the Official Secrets Act. The scope of the Official Secrets Act 1911 had been extended in 1920 to incorporate elements of the Defence of the Realm Act 1914 which had heralded a remarkable increase in central state power.[23] Nevertheless, Loseby's concerns were shared by others and J.H. Thomas, Labour MP for Derby, who captured the mood of the House when he said, 'there is no department of public life and no body of public servants in this country whose reputation this House of Commons ought [sic] more jealously guard than the civil service.'[24] Loseby's questions and claims then had caused considerable alarm prompting Parliament to rush through the Tribunals legislation as the requisite device to deal with the problem.

There had been, since 1918, a persistent and underlying fear that there was 'corruption in certain government departments in the handling of great sums of money and the rumours should be laid low on behalf of the great body of civil servants which we are proud to know is honest and can be trusted'.[25] Some MPs and Lords though feared that the Tribunals would become a permanent feature which could represent a 'serious breach of [citizens'] constitutional rights'.[26] The spectre of a court of Star Chamber was more troubling, apparently, than the trading of honours by Freddy Guest and Maundy Gregory on behalf of Lloyd George's election fund. The full implications of the fund did not become clear until the following year, 1922, and in any case both the Liberals and Conservatives were beneficiaries of the fund and therefore had no motive to expose the issue. Thus, the Tribunal system was established as a consequence of what historians might judge to be a sideshow compared with the sale of honours to fund political parties.

The debate concerning Tribunals was conflated with misgivings about the increasing powers of the state as signified by the government's proposals to extend the scope of the Official Secrets legislation with a new bill. The febrile atmosphere created by the emergencies of war was sustained in the years after 1918, and it had certainly pervaded the debate on the Official Secrets Bill in 1920. Sir Donald MacLean, a leading Liberal in the Asquith group, tackled the Government's Bill from a classic Liberal position: there was growing concern that the power of the state was increasing inordinately. He went further arguing that the Bill would give the executive 'war power in peace time to destroy the liberties of the subject'.[27] Whether the Tribunals Act represented a similar increase in state power can of course be debated, but there was growing apprehension about the growth of an overmighty state. Such a view remained a major impediment to reform until after 1979.

The subsequent inquiry into the activities of the Ministry of Munitions was chaired by Lord Cave, the later Lord Chancellor, but found, remarkably, there was no case of corruption to be answered. Thereafter, the Tribunal system was used in matters connected with corruption as it affected police forces – the Metropolitan Police in 1925 and the police forces of Kilmarnock and St. Helens in 1925 and 1928, respectively. The St. Helen's case was particularly intriguing since it revealed the mischief that might arise once a Chief Constable was at odds with the local Watch Committee. The Chief Constable, Arthur Ellerington, was accused by the Watch Committee of numerous misdemeanours, but significantly these also included allegations of corruption in that he had used his public office for the 'private advantage of himself and his friends'. He had secured the delivery of coal to his private house during a coal dispute and had also employed a police constable as a general servant in his own home. Additionally, he had arranged for repairs of motor cars for himself and a local doctor by fire station mechanics. The use of public resources for private use was perhaps one of the most camouflaged examples of corruption. Fortunately for Ellerington, the Watch Committee's procedures were flawed, and its attempt to force him into retirement was highly irregular. Ellerington was reinstated and the Tribunal concluded that his 'honour' was intact.[28] The establishment of the Tribunal system then provides a key into the problem of corruption and the misuse of public resources by public office holders. Corruption was of concern from the beginning of the period, but a critique of corruption evolved only gradually over the sixty-five years under review.

The debate about corruption was informed first by the imperial ethic and the civilising mission that went with it. These ideas were underpinned of course by the ideas of British liberalism which extolled the rule of law but with minimal intervention by the state. The crisis of the Great War, the rise of a radical right in many parts of Europe and an encroaching communism promoted by the Union of Soviet Socialist Republics (USSR) seemed to place the liberal state in great danger. It has been suggested that the kind of state which confined itself to providing the ground rules of business and civil society, police and prisons as well as armed forces to keep danger at bay was essentially a 'night watchman state' that would become 'obsolete' as the statist parties in Europe advanced.[29] British political leaders and other members of the elite accepted Britain's imperial role. Statements about corruption in Britain itself were invariably qualified by the claim that Britain was not a corrupt country and that the problem of corruption was more prevalent elsewhere. Such a view fitted with the British elite's world view which had been constructed as part of the imperial mission. The notion that corruption was something that happened elsewhere, overseas, was deeply ingrained in British assumptions about their civilising mission to teach the virtues of British institutions to other peoples of the world. Thus, Lord Lloyd speaking at a meeting of the Indian Empire Society in Exeter in 1934 asserted that 'whenever, Parliamentary Government had been tried in the East it had led to chaos or tyranny [and] in India local government invariably spelled corruption'.[30] It was not surprising then that episodes of corruption at home were apprehended with a deep-seated concern. The sense of outrage from social and political leaders was characterised by a stern disapprobation. Given such a frame of mind, the impulse to promote reform was ill-developed as it tried to assert the primacy of an individual's conduct which was informed by a moral code that encompassed duty, trust, honour and pride in the British way of doing things, but the press and politicians could only ventilate their concerns about corruption in terms of lost reputation. In Glasgow then, the press reported in 1929 about rumours that had begun to circulate about the affairs of Glasgow's Corporation, and the editors of the *Glasgow Evening News* and the *Glasgow Herald* waged a campaign against the Corporation. In the council chamber itself, John McGovern, the radical Independent Labour Party (ILP) councillor and MP weighed in: 'The civic administration of Glasgow was once the pride of the world, and we hope this inquiry will bring to light any disgraceful actions that might have been taken in the city'. Wrapping himself in the shibboleth of Victorian liberalism he extolled the virtues of trust and duty and he hoped that it was an opportunity to 'clean up the city'.[31]

The imperial legacy and the preservation of reputation were intimately linked. For example, in 1907 the Bribery and Secret Commissions Prevention

League had been founded. Its major supporters were businessmen and aristocrats who linked the problems of corruption and secret commissions (payments) with problems of international trade and the maintenance of Empire. One of its leading figures was Lord Inchcape, a Scottish shipping magnate, who had sat on the first Tribunal of Inquiry which investigated alleged corruption in the Ministry of Munitions in 1921. The Prevention League acted as a pressure group to bring cases of corruption to public attention. Its membership probably peaked at around 370 members in 1913.[32] However, even after 1918 it continued to attract support from MPs, barristers, retired judges and middle class organisations such as rotary clubs. It acted as a self-appointed watchdog, reporting the number of corruption cases brought before the courts as well as acting as a lobby group. Arguably its greatest success was securing the support of Holford Knight, MP for South Nottingham, who moved the consolidation clause to amend the Local Government Act 1929 and include a requirement that councillors declare their interests in matters of contracts and planning.[33] It also carried its campaign to the international stage submitting its reports and proposals to the Economic Council of the League of Nations and called for anti-bribery and anti-corruption measures to be adopted by all 'civilised countries'.[34] Just as Lord Snell, chairman of the London County Council (LCC) subscribed to the virtues promoted by the Clarendon Commissioners when reporting on Nine Great Public Schools in 1864, so the leading spokesman of the Prevention of Corruption League articulated his concerns in typically Anglocentric terms. Lord Crewe, a former Secretary of State for India and Chairman of the LCC in 1917, speaking at a League luncheon at the Savoy Hotel in 1929 expressed, neatly, the imperial conception of the corruption issue: 'through the history of all countries down to the most modern development of civilisation in these days when the terms "graft" and "boodle" were brought to us from overseas, we could trace a perpetual existence of the taking of secret commissions'.[35]

'Graft' and 'boodle' were American terms, and Crewe's use of them indicated a growing interest in the problems of corruption apparently so prevalent in American politics: the writings of the muckraking journalists of the United States including Lincoln Steffens[36] were becoming increasingly well known outside America. Lord Crewe was also supported in this view by Lord Inchcape: 'in India and other countries ... bribery is so deep-rooted and so common that familiarity tempted some to condone the depravity. It is a matter of pride that this country should have been the first to try to prevent bribery and corruption by special legislation. There are special laws or ordinances against bribery, nearly all over the British Empire'. In addition to the assumptions shaped by Britain's imperial role, the critique of corruption as it evolved in the 1930s was also informed by the twin themes of the civic tradition and the notion of civic pride that went with it. Inherited from the city fathers of the nineteenth century, the idea of the city was imbued with a lofty idealism and dignity that had stirred a reforming spirit: 'Religion and history came into the picture at many points. The King James Bible spoke usually of cities not of towns. It could be used to point to the need both for civic obligation and social reform. The experience of both the Greek *polis* and the Renaissance city-state was held up for study and emulation'.[37] However, episodes of corruption punctured that idealism. At the *Glasgow Tribunal*, for example, the Chairman, Lord Anderson, in his closing remarks repeated the injunction made by Sir Godfrey Collins: 'Let all those whose whisperings and stories have suggested that allegations of corruption exist now come forward and show the same civic spirit as Mrs McArthur [a key witness], or for evermore keep silent'.[38]

The traditions of imperial thinking and the idealistic and liberal notions that lay behind the British civic tradition – public spirit, puritanical virtue and selflessness – were significant inhibitors to the development of a structured reform programme. Additionally, intellectual thought in the interwar years was drenched in assumptions about the imminent collapse of civilisation, and perhaps not unsurprisingly, British intellectuals of diverse persuasions held up the city and Britain's version of municipal government as a beacon of light as it signalled progress and reform.[39] Moreover, the Tribunals were primarily investigative bodies and did not, initially, make recommendations for reform. Thus, although the Glasgow investigation was thorough and wide ranging, neither the Secretary of State for Scotland nor Glasgow Corporation acted upon its findings. To the blend of the imperial civilising mission and the civic tradition were added a further set of ideas that emanated from the incipient town planning movement. Patrick Geddes had developed his thinking into a theory of civics which was related to ideas about citizenship and the way in which enlightened individuals might contribute to the life of their local city. The contributory strands were found in the ideas of the settlement movement and in the housing reform movement, and they were taken up by Ernest Simon and Eva Hubback who promoted the idea of education for citizenship. These ideas were essentially utopian and assumed that the well-being, good order and harmony of society and the city would be somehow the natural consequence of the interaction of citizens with their environment. In this case, good citizenship was the antidote to corruption. The exponents and followers of these beliefs had little to offer when faced with the dysfunctional and antisocial behaviours of the corrupt.

The consequences of the *Glasgow Tribunal* were significant in the sense that the civic tradition which had characterised the Victorian city was now a hollow shell. Thus, when Glasgow's Corporation attempted to promote a municipal savings bank and to establish its own tram and motor body manufacturing company, its parliamentary bill was defeated. The arguments of the Glasgow MPs who promoted the measure were easily rebuffed by the government. First Secretary to the Treasury, Duff-Cooper, was dismissive of the proposal damning the Corporation's plans with faint praise:

> We all recognised and admire that civic spirit, but there is nothing more unfortunate than when the civic spirit of a great city is misled because that may lead to disaster. Anybody who studies history, not the ancient history but the recent history,

of other countries, say of France and America, know the awful misfortunes which have befallen great cities owing to bad administration which creeps more easily into municipal government, than into the government of a great State. It is therefore dangerous to rely too much upon the civic spirit of a community to support ... their elected governors – temporarily elected governors – and to give powers which may not, in the long run, be used for people's good.[40]

Duff-Cooper's distinction between local municipal government and the government of the national state was a sleight of hand to avoid imputations that might be levelled against the national political elite. Glasgow's fall from grace as a progressive and reforming city marked by civic probity was undoubtedly shocking to contemporaries. Further, the later intransigence of the Corporation meant that there were further corruption episodes in 1941, in 1968 and again in 1990.

If the years from 1929 to 1939 were marked by an inability of reformers to put forward a cogent plan of reform to control corruption, the outbreak of the Second World War might have been expected to change the dynamic. In some respects, it did. The lessons of the First World War were not forgotten, and the state quickly ratcheted up the scale of its intervention. Conscription, direction of the economy, rationing, censorship of the press and internment of civilians regarded as enemies of the state represented a significant redrawing of the relationship between the state and the citizen. The undeclared contract between the citizen and the state meant that the former accepted compulsory measures in pursuit of victory and the latter agreed to make provision for the economic and social welfare of the citizenry. It found its emblematic expression in the Beveridge Report in 1942. Beveridge had many allies – J.M. Keynes, Archbishop William Temple, J.B. Priestley, George Orwell, the Labour Party and the Tory Reform Group – all of whom were advocates of a more interventionist state. There was opposition, however, from such as the Progress Trust and the National League for Freedom, and they received intellectual nourishment from Friedrich Hayek, the Austrian economist based at the LSE since 1931. For Hayek, state planning and control would result in 'corruption, tyranny and totalitarianism'.[41] These ideas would be elaborated later in Hayek's *The Road to Serfdom* published in 1944. The significance of Hayek's thinking was not realised until the Thatcher government after 1979 when local government became increasingly marginalised by a powerful *dirigiste* central government.

The privations experienced by the population during and after the War provided an ideal incubation unit for the culture of corrupt behaviour. Two instances can suffice. In Newcastle in 1944, the Home Secretary, Herbert Morrison, set up a Tribunal to investigate allegations of corruption in the city. Councillor Richard Embleton had amassed considerable power through the accumulation of numerous offices. The Tribunal's conclusions were forthright asserting that Embleton, by virtue of his position as Chairman of the Emergency

Committee and holding the office of Deputy Controller of Air Raid Precautions (ARP), was able to 'enforce his will in a way that would have been impossible if he had not been Chairman'.[42] Further, he had regularly acted in contravention of the Local Government Act 1933 in that he had spoken and voted on matters in which he had a direct pecuniary interest. He had flagrantly bought, using public funds, police horses and used them for his own riding and pleasure even having himself photographed by one of the police grooms using police photographic equipment and materials. Remarkably, however, the Tribunal concluded that there had not been any corruption, but then required Embleton's resignation.[43]

The Tribunal was less concerned with individual culpability and instead concentrated its fire on the failure of Newcastle City Council's systems of control being especially concerned with the arrangements for delegated authority. The Newcastle-upon-Tyne Improvement Act 1882 enabled the council to delegate powers to its various chairmen. This was a common practice elsewhere, but in Newcastle's case, unlike the LCC's standing orders, there was no facility for a councillor, except as an individual, to seek referral of a subcommittee matter to the full council.[44] The habit of annual renewal without challenge or question was probably in reality a consequence of a shortage of willing volunteers, the ability and esteem in which a particular councillor might be regarded by his fellow councillors, or just simple inertia. Gentlemanly politics may also have meant that other councillors were reluctant to challenge a chairman's re-election for fear of the 'odium' that might befall the councillor who challenged re-election. The consequences though were considerable for the general patterns of deference that prevailed often meant that the chairman's view went unchallenged. Embleton had flourished within a culture where every man in the fire brigade and the police force considered that his wishes had to be met. This was not only accepted by constables, sergeants and ordinary firemen but also by the Chief Constable and successive Superintendents of the Fire Brigade.[45] Despite the equivocal conclusion on matters of individual culpability, Herbert Morrison was clear: Embleton and Crawley, the Chief Constable, had to go. He had also written to the Newcastle Watch Committee asking it to consider the merit of the Chief Constable's continuation in post. Embleton bowed to the pressure and resigned not only from the Watch Committee but also the council.[46]

Newcastle's arrangements in respect of financial control were also found wanting, and the Tribunal recommended that regulations concerning the sale and disposal of assets, the payments made to contractors, arrangements in respect of accounts and the maintenance of inventories and audit all needed to be overhauled. It also recommended the establishment of a central purchasing department.[47] Thus, the *Newcastle Tribunal Report* was significant in that it inched towards more regulatory control of an essentially technical and bureaucratic nature. The actions of one man and the collusion of other pliant high status officers had brought Newcastle City Council into disrepute. *The Times* editorial followed the lead of the Tribunal asserting that the findings of the Inquiry served as a 'reproach to the local government of an important city'. It invoked the general slackness of administration and the damage to the city's reputation.[48] The ideal of a 'fit and proper person' had seemingly been sullied. Embleton's cavalier attitudes to signing petrol coupons had been his undoing. His activities and the general lack of accountability and the culture of trust had enabled him to enjoy the high life from probably as early as 1937 until 1944. The Tribunal went much further than its predecessors and perhaps signified not just the determination of the Home Secretary but also a new climate that would herald a more interventionist approach to the problem of corruption.

The Lynskey Tribunal (1948) investigated claims that a minister at the Board of Trade, John Belcher, and, George Gibson, a Director of the Bank of England had accepted bribes from Sidney Stanley who presented himself as a proto-lobbyist. In the event, Stanley was shown to be a trickster using several false names, variously Koszynski, Wulkan and Blotz, and who sought to impress, but he had lavished hospitality on both Belcher and Gibson. Given the robust approach of the Newcastle Inquiry and the apparent puritanical zeal of Attlee's government, it might have been expected that an equally tough approach would have been exercised. It has been observed that Attlee's post-war Cabinet presented an 'earnest and high minded [image] scrupulous about keeping election pledges, keen to keep the state machine uncorrupted, and constitutionally correct'.[49] In Cabinet discussion, however, the members of the Labour government were clearly more circumspect. Herbert Morrison observed, 'Corruption in public life is the great danger to democracy. Lucky we haven't had much of it. Where it exists, the largest difficulty is always proof. For all participants are interested to keep it in the dark'. Aneurin Bevan was particularly acute to the political dangers exposed by the Belcher case and did not wish for a debate prior to an election as it would 'invite muckraking'. However, James Chuter-Ede believed that local officials in local government did have considerable power in relation to planning and that there were dangers there. Such a division of opinion was an invitation for Attlee to do nothing.[50] The consequence of Belcher was that Hartley Shawcross, the Attorney General, came forward with proposals that the matter of public licences and permits issued by the Board of Trade should be subject to criminal procedures.[51] The Cabinet discussed the matter again in May 1949 but concluded that 'intent' was difficult to prove in corruption cases. Interest in the issue fizzled out, and in the following year, the Cabinet asserted that the 1916 Act was sufficient.[52] The unwillingness to come forward with new measures was encouraged by a deep-seated resistance to opening up a public debate on the matter for fear that the press might use it as a signal to bring forward more examples of wrongdoing. Herbert Morrison was especially forthright here, as lobby journalists could 'cast a slur upon an honourable body of men'.[53]

The main fallout from Lynskey's investigation of Belcher, Gibson and Stanley was a prosecution of Sherman's Pools, but Harold Wilson, President of the Board of Trade, withdrew the summons when the Stipendiary Magistrate hearing the case died. Wilson was challenged in the House but retorted that there had already been enough publicity and that 'substantial justice had already been done' and that further costs were unjustified.[54] Sidney Stanley, Belcher's corrupter, was a Polish Jewish émigré who had made good during the War particularly with the Ministry of Supply manufacturing clothing for the forces. He was a colourful character who, because of these dealings with a government department, thought that he could set himself up as a 'contact man'.[55] He was an illegal immigrant and had various scrapes with the law including bankruptcy and fraud. The Home Office had sought to deport him but had lost track of him because of his various name changes. He fled to the recently established state of Israel. Following Belcher's and Gibson's resignations, parliament established an investigative committee to examine the role of so-called 'intermediaries' which concluded that there had always been agents, contact men and fixers, but following the Lynskey Tribunal, the Committee also sought to 'examine how far persons are making a business of acting as intermediaries between government departments and the public and to report whether by the activities of such persons give rise to abuses'. The Committee was also concerned to discover whether the activities of intermediaries had reached proportions that constituted a 'new social phenomenon'.[56] It recognised that the Board of Trade was particularly complex and its purview included imports, exports, manufacture, raw materials, regional distribution and company insurance. The potential for corrupt behaviour and Stanley's claims that he could procure licences and concessions was a clear indication of the potential for corruption. He was involved in numerous activities but particularly to import fairground equipment from the United States including fruit machines and pinball machines. The Committee identified numerous areas of government that might attract intermediaries. They included the Admiralty, the Inland Revenue, the Ministry of Supply, the Ministry of Works and the Home Office. John Poulson admitted later that it was in his dealings with the Ministry of Supply and the Ministry of Works that he recognised the potential to make money. Remarkably, the Committee concluded that there was little of concern. Instead, its main focus was on the Home Office where it appeared that there were intermediaries active in the process of applications for naturalisation from refugees and immigrants. It was claimed that many of these individuals were 'scarcely reputable'.[57] It concluded that many individuals seeking naturalisation were especially vulnerable to the 'unscrupulous'. The potential for bribery and corruption was already well known, and the case of Stanley Briggs, a Home Office immigration clerk, who accepted more than £900 in bribes as a means of paying off his own debts illustrated the problem. Briggs went to prison for twelve months. The Recorder passing sentence on Briggs revealed the latent anxiety that prevailed on the matter of immigration coupled with bribery and corruption: 'corruption is a most insidious thing. It is a cancer in the heart of commercial activities and when it creeps in liberty and even justice depart. It is essential that a man occupying an official position should not abuse it as you have done'.[58] The Belcher–Stanley affair only served to feed the misgivings that prevailed in political circles concerning immigration. The idea that the area of immigration and naturalisation was prey to intermediaries deploying corrupt methods then smacked of incipient racism or was a function of the legacy of imperialism. It was at least alarm at the dramatic increase in naturalisation certificates granted by the Home Office: in the period 1931–40, there had been more than 15,000 naturalisations, but by 1941–50, this had increased more than threefold to over 50,000.

The post-war consensus to rebuild Britain socially encapsulated in the principles of the Beveridge Report and physically because of war damage and long-term neglect of the housing stock drew central and local government into an ever closer partnership. It was a relationship which was to prove remarkably durable but was also a significant inhibition to reforming the corruption laws in relation to public bodies such as local authorities. There were instances of corruption in post-war Britain, but these were often given scant attention. This was certainly the case in respect of revelations of corruption in St. Helens and Liverpool in 1946–47 even though Liverpool was at that time under Conservative control.[59] It was possible that Labour's reluctance to pursue instances of corruption, even when perpetrated by the Conservatives, was born of the fact that it was highly sensitive to the issue of its own relation with the co-operative movement which sponsored many MPs. In this sense, the co-operative organisation occupied a client relationship with the Labour Party where the Party was reluctant to punish loyalty. In some towns and cities, Labour was in the majority on the local council, and many local Labour councillors were also co-operators, with shares and dividends. Were they potentially compromised if they failed to declare an interest when speaking or voting on such matters as land purchase and retail development where a local authority and the Co-operative Society were in negotiations? Attlee's cabinet debated the issue at length, and Herbert Morrison feared any relaxation of the law on this matter saying that 'small traders, may say we are discriminating in favour of our supporters'. The issue had assumed significant proportions in Scunthorpe where all but four councillors were members of the Co-operative Society. The Scunthorpe Labour Councillors had been challenged on the probity of their actions when dealing with matters that had affected co-operative premises and sought to meet with the prime minister himself. Nye Bevan spoke out strongly against such a meeting and that the government should not be seen to 'be weakening the law on corruption'.[60]

Even after 1951 when the Conservatives returned to power, there was little motive to change the law in relation to corruption. Perhaps it was not necessary as many of the cases reported were apparently petty, or so-called 'white' corruption, such as the Blackpool businessman who provided counting machines for turnstiles at the Festival of Britain and attempted to bribe civil servants[61] or the case of Wilfred Ring, Chairman of the Library and Museum Committee of Hove Town Council, who sold his own produce (seaside souvenirs) through the town's museum.[62] Venues of entertainment and leisure may have been peculiarly susceptible to corrupt dealings as the case of Arthur Salisbury, a Blackpool alderman and former mayor, who failed to declare his interest when the town corporation bought land adjacent to his own commercial garage.[63] The local Liberals pursued the matter with some vigour but were unable to make any political capital from the case. Matters in London were probably more problematic when police officers were discovered to have procured bribes to turn a blind eye on a range of vice offences in 1955.[64] Nevertheless, corruption continued to feature on the cabinet's radar throughout the post-war years: in 1948, Ernest Bevin raised concerns about the possibility of bribery having been involved in British Overseas Airways Corporation's (BOAC) purchase of the Ambassador aircraft.[65] The BOAC case highlighted a danger that was to become increasingly significant over time: competition amongst corporate businesses especially where it converged with the interests of the state would become another source of corruption.

The legacy of wartime too left its indelible marks. This was the case with the Crichel Down affair in 1954. Part of a country estate had been purchased by the War Office in 1942 but later transferred to the Ministry of Agriculture who had sought to sell it off at its market value much to the dismay of its former owners who sought to buy it back. The matter was investigated by Sir Andrew Clark QC who concluded that there was 'no trace in this case of anything of the nature of bribery, corruption or personal dishonesty'.[66] A subsequent public inquiry recommended change in the law, and the Minister for Agriculture, Sir Thomas Dugdale, resigned. Although it was probably not a case of corruption but more a matter of maladministration, Norman Brook, Secretary to the Cabinet from 1947, asserted that the Crichel Down case raised an important question in respect of public confidence in the civil service for which 'incorruptibility and efficiency [were] two obvious requirements'.[67] In many respects, however, the problems of domestic corruption seemed small change in the matters of state. Imperial rundown and the threat of communism loomed larger with an ongoing debate about corruption overseas in the Gold Coast, Nigeria, Portugal, Greece, Spain, Egypt and Iran. It was perhaps ironic against that background that the government resolved to establish an Overseas Information Service as it was believed that Britain could offer a 'distinctive contribution to shaping world society'.[68] The persistence of assumptions about its world role meant that Britain's politicians faced no driving dynamic to change the law in respect of corruption. In the meantime, instances of corruption were to be left to the courts and magistrates and judges to hold the moral line. Thus, Sir Gerald Dodson, the Middlesex Recorder passing sentence in a case of bribery to obtain a council flat at Stamford Hill in north London, asserted the following: 'I want it to be understood that these days corruption is sapping the life out of the community. If it goes on in the national life will disintegrate as surely as that of other empires which have preceded us, for no community can exist when the heart of it is eaten out by corruption. This is why this case is as grave as it is'.[69]

For the period after 1945 down to the mid-1960s, there was little commitment to reform the laws in relation to corruption or indeed to make the activities of local government more open to public scrutiny. For example, in November 1959, the new MP for Finchley, Margaret Thatcher, introduced a bill to make council meetings including subcommittees open to the public; Thatcher was advised by Dame Evelyn Sharp that the Department 'had in mind to agree a "code of behaviour" with the representatives of local authorities in an effort to get the position satisfactory without legislation'.[70] Nevertheless, Thatcher pressed forward with the Public Bodies (Admission of the Press to Meetings) Bill in November 1959. It was in fact a partisan attack on Labour-controlled local authorities. Nevertheless, she had hit on a peculiarly British problem – secrecy in public life.[71] She encountered stern opposition from various local government associations, but the Public Bodies (Admissions to Meetings) Act 1960 extended public and press rights to be admitted to council meetings. However, it was not in fact until the 1970s in the wake of the Poulson scandal that a more coherent response to the problem of corruption came to be formulated: Lord Redcliffe-Maud had been asked by Edward Heath to investigate problems in local government in 1973, the *Prime Minister's Committee on Local Government Rules of Conduct*, and he reported in 1974. The recommendations were wide ranging and comprehensive, stressing the importance of honesty amongst public office holders in order to create public confidence. Specifically, Redcliffe-Maud recommended strengthening the law in respect of pecuniary interests and their declaration by councillors. Further, local authorities should be required to maintain a register of interests and the Corruption Act of 1916 amended to encompass the awarding of council contracts. Additionally, he recommended the establishment of a code of conduct for all councillors.[72] The *Royal Commission on Standards of Conduct* chaired by Lord Salmon was equally wide ranging, but its effectiveness was compromised by the disagreement between Lords Houghton and Salmon. The former believed that 'this mischief [corruption] lies at the numerous meeting points along the boundary between public service and private interests'. Houghton recognised correctly the importance of urban redevelopment and its role in the economy: 'During the 1960s the coming together of planners, developers and even architects, property owners, contractors and local authorities provided all the basic ingredients of corruption – capital gains, competitive enterprise, business profits and rapidly expanding public works. With such large interests at stake in the many hundreds of millions of pounds of public expenditure involved, it is not surprising that corruption has been discovered'.[73]

Nevertheless, both reports recognised the onerous workloads borne by committee chairmen and favoured a more generous system of allowances. Tightening the rules on tendering for contracts was also acknowledged as a significant measure to control corruption. Redcliffe-Maud, too, advocated better allowance system but was against payment since that would, he thought, 'change the tradition of unpaid service unless public opinion crystallises or it becomes clear that the new system is likely to impose a wholly new burden on councillors' time'.[74] He also favoured the abolition of aldermen as they were a potential source of oligarchy. Ultimately though he appreciated 'there are no votes in local government reform. All party managers will warn against it'.[75] Local government had in fact become paralysed by inertia, and Redcliffe-Maud warned, 'If we fail here, and stay put with the system inherited from 1888 local government will be discredited within the next ten years'. He went on to identify key urban issues – homelessness, urban regeneration and conservation of the countryside arguing that they were 'too serious to be left to local councillors, and we shall loose our heritage of local freedom'.[76]

The 1970s was a crucial decade in respect of the reputation of local government. The Poulson case was the fulcrum around which the attitude of national politicians turned as they saw a means not necessarily of reforming the conduct of local councillors but rather reducing, wholesale, the power and responsibilities of local authorities. Margaret Thatcher became leader of the Conservatives in 1975, and with the guidance of her *eminence grise*, Sir Keith Joseph, she engineered a significant shift in Conservative attitudes to local government. Traditionally, Conservatives had been the friends of local government. Now, with the evaporation of the post-war consensus, the Conservatives under Thatcher's leadership, Conservatism came to a new position which was to equate state size with individual freedom. A smaller state left more room for wealth creation and less regulation also implied, in the minds of those who followed Hayek's dictum, less corruption. Further, the populist platform for better value for money from public services was a powerful rallying cry: 'No one who has lived in this country during the last five years can fail to be aware how the balance of our society has been increasingly tilted in favour of the state at the expense of individual freedom'.[77] She would reduce 'waste, bureaucracy and over-government' and attacked plans by Southwark Borough to build a new town hall for £50 million. Once in power, she launched a full-scale assault on local government. In part, this was inspired by party animus, but the creation of new devices – the Housing Corporation and Urban Development Corporations – created new sources of patronage and corruption. Ivor Crewe in his evidence to Nolan pointed out that there was growing public suspicion of government use of quangos in place of local authorities. He had carried out his own survey and discovered that there were thirty-four wives of Conservative MPs as against only two Labour wives adding mischievously that he could not explain 'the discrepancy on meritocratic grounds alone'. This was certainly a form of patrimonialism. He thought the old consensus had now been replaced by a new 'corporate political culture'.[78] At the same time, a new voracious appetite for power had developed perhaps most vividly exemplified by Dame Shirley Porter, the Conservative leader of Westminster City Council. Her win-at-all-costs approach to local elections caused her to fall foul of the District Auditor who severely criticised her for her abuse of the 'right to buy' scheme in respect of council housing. Thus, local government had fallen from grace. Attempts at reform had at best been slow to develop, and public disinterest and cynicism had contributed to such a state of affairs. One witness to Nolan poured derision on local government saying, 'people who become councillors are usually retired, unemployed against their will, or the spouses of rich husbands or wives whom they can rely on to support them'.[79] Moreover, the problems recognised by Lord Salmon were recapitulated by Lord Nolan twenty years on: 'where there is a long term overwhelming majority for a single party, councillors are not subject to the full democratic process, serve for too long without real accountability and either enjoy excessively close relationships with senior officers or exercise too much authority over them'.[80] Thus, local government was at its lowest ebb, and corruption had been a critical factor in that outcome.

The Nolan Commission sought to resuscitate the ethical principles that lay behind the Victorian liberal notion of a fit and proper person with a regular incantation of the Seven Principles of Public Life: selflessness, integrity, objectivity, accountability, openness, honesty and leadership. It was an attempt to re-establish an ethical framework that had seemingly been mislaid by the legatees of the Victorian liberal system. There should be a code of conduct for councillors but developed by individual councils. Each council should have its own Standards Committee with the authority to discipline 'errant councillors'. The establishment of local government tribunals to act as arbiters in respect of a local council's code of conduct was also promoted. Finally, the designation of 'misuse of public office' was perhaps the most radical proposal.[81] Like Stanley in search of Livingston, Nolan went in search of liberalism's maps and charts that navigated the passage towards a new ethical public life. The Seven Principles were emblazoned on all the publications of the Commission. They were even produced on plastic wallet-sized cards and given to all new MPs and councillors, as type of 'ethical credit card'.[82] Despite Nolan's efforts and those of his successors, Transparency International's Corruption Perception Index shows that Britain's standing in the world has sunk: ranked twelfth in 1995 and above Germany and Japan, it dropped to twentieth in 2010 and below Ireland, Germany and Japan. It had made a modest recovery by 2011 when it ranked seventeenth. Overall though its stock of credit in the ethics stakes has declined, and this has been due in part by a lack of political will to confront the challenge.

Notes

1 *Prime Minister's Committee on Local Government Rules of Conduct* (1974), Cmnd., 5636, para. 1, p. vii.
2 Lord Blake, evidence to *Standards of Conduct in Public Life* (1995), Cm., 2850-II, para. 65.
3 Doig, A., 'From Lynskey to Nolan: the corruption of British politics and public service', *Journal of the Law Society*, 23: 1 (1996), pp. 35–6.
4 Searle, G., *Corruption in British Politics 1995–1930* (Oxford: Clarendon Press, 1987).
5 *Local Government Chronicle*, 21 January 1994.
6 *The Guardian*, 20, 22, 25 October 1994.
7 *The Guardian*, 17 September 1994, 11 January 1996.
8 Doig, A., *Corruption and Misconduct in Contemporary British Politics* (London: Harmondsworth Penguin, 1984), pp. 387–401.
9 *Prime Minister's Committee*, Cmd., 5636, para. 1, p. vii.
10 Gildea, R., *France Since 1945* (Oxford: Oxford University Press, 1997), p. 197.
11 Ginsborg, *Italy and Its Discontents*, pp. 193–4.
12 Hoggart, R., *Uses of Literacy* (London: Penguin, 1957), p. 280.
13 Langford, P., *A Polite and Commercial People, England 1727–1783* (Oxford: Oxford University Press, 1989), p. 716.
14 Neild, R., *Public Corruption: The Dark Side of Social Evolution* (London: Anthem, 2002), pp. 15–19.
15 Oborne, P., *Triumph of the Political Class* (London: Pocket Books, 2007), pp. 55–7.
16 O'Leary, C., *The Elimination of Corrupt Practices in British Elections 1886–1911* (Oxford: Clarendon Press, 1962).
17 Bew, P., *Ireland: The Politics of Enmity 1789–2006* (Oxford: Oxford University Press, 2007).
18 *The Times*, 18 March 1919.
19 *The Times*, 16 April 1920.
20 *The Times*, 5 April 1920.
21 *Hansard*, HC Debates, 22 February 1921, vol. 138, cc. 767–70.
22 *Hansard*, HC Debates, 22 February 1921, vol. 138, cc. 863–86.
23 Vincent, D., *The Culture of Secrecy: Britain 1832–1998* (Oxford: Oxford University Press, 1998), pp. 172–4.
24 *Hansard*, HC Debates, 22 February 1921, vol. 138, cc. 863–86.
25 *Ibid.*, James Seddon MP (Stoke-on-Trent, Hanley)., Ibid., 863–86.
26 *The Times*, 17 March 1921, Letter from William Bull M.P.
27 *Ibid.*
28 *Tribunal of Inquiry, Charges Against the Chief Constable of St. Helens* (1928), Cmd., 3103.
29 Hobsbawm, E., *Age of Extremes* (London: Michael Joseph, 1994), p. 140.
30 *The Times*, 25 May 1934.
31 *Hansard*, HC Debates, 10 April 1933, vol. 276, cc. 2336–42.
32 *The Times*, 26 February 1913.
33 *Nottingham Evening Post*, 9 April 1934; *The Times*, 22 February 1935.
34 *The Times*, 26 February 1926.
35 *The Times*, 19 December 1929.

36 Steffens, L., *The Shame of the Cities* (New York: Hill and Wang, 1904) was a collection of Steffens' numerous reports exposing corruption in numerous American cities including Philadelphia, Boston and New York.

37 Briggs, A., *Victorian Cities* (London: Harmondsworth Penguin, 1963), pp. 32–3.

38 *Glasgow Tribunal Inquiry* (1933), Appendix 15.

39 Overy, R., *The Morbid Age: Britain and the Crisis of Civilisation, 1919–1939* (London: Penguin, 2010), pp. 32–3.

40 *The Scotsman*, 27 March 1935; *Hansard*, HC Debates., vol. 299, cc. 1820–77.

41 Donelly, M., *Britain in the Second World War* (Routledge, Abingdon, 1999), p. 45; Cockett, R., *Thinking the Unthinkable: Think Tanks and the Economic Counter-Revolution* (London: Harper Collins, 1995), pp. 57–99.

42 *Glasgow Tribunal*, para. 316, p. 56.

43 *The Times*, 30 March 1944.

44 *Glasgow Tribunal*, para. 333, p. 58.

45 *Ibid.*, para. 326, p. 57.

46 *The Times*, 3 May 1944.

47 *Glasgow Tribunal*, para. 337, p. 59.

48 *The Times*, 3 May 1944.

49 Harrison, B., *Seeking a Role: The United Kingdom 1951–1970* (Oxford: Clarendon Press, 2009), p. 60; Hennessy, P., *The Prime Minister: The Office and Its Holders since 1945* (London: Allen Lane, 2000), p. 169.

50 NA, CAB 195/7, 27 January 1949, Cabinet Secretary's Notebook: Minutes and Papers.

51 CAB 129/34, 6 April 1949.

52 CAB 128/15, 9 May 1949; CAB195/8, 23 November 1950.

53 CAB 129/22, 26 November 1947.

54 *Hansard*, HC Debates, 13 May 1948, vol. 450, cc. 236–7.

55 Barron, S., *The Contact Man: The Story of Sidney Stanley and the Lynskey Tribunal* (London: Secker and Warburg, 1966).

56 *Report of the Committee on Intermediaries* (1950), Cmd., 7904, p. 6.

57 *Ibid.*, para. 186, p. 62.

58 *The Times*, 5 May 1938.

59 NA, CAB 195/5, Cabinet Secretary's Notebook, 4 February 1947.

60 NA, CAB 195/5, previously CM 94(47), 11 December 1947.

61 *The Times*, 15 March 1952.

62 *The Times*, 15 October 1954.

63 *The Times*, 5 May 1956, 10 August 1956.

64 *The Times*, 22 November 1955.

65 NA, CAB 195/6, Cabinet Secretary's Notebook, 29 July 1948.

66 NA, CAB 129/68, Cabinet Memorandum- Sir Andrew Clark's Report, 1 June 1954. Griffiths, J., 'Crichel down – the most famous farm in British Constitutional History', *Contemporary British History*, 1: 1 (1987), pp. 35–40.

67 NA, CAB 129/69, Cabinet Memorandum, Crichel Down, 19 July 1954.

68 NA, CAB 129/87, Cabinet Memorandum: Overseas Information Service, 18 June 1957.

69 *The Times*, 28 October 1948.

70 NA 1959–60: Private Members Bill HLG 29/490, Dame Evelyn Sharp's Minute 2, December 1959.

71 Vincent, *Culture of Secrecy*; Heather Brooke, *Silent State* (London: Windmill Books, 2010).

72 *Prime Minister's Committee*, Cmd., 5636, para. 18, p. ix.

73 *Royal Commission on Standards of Conduct in Public Life* (1976), Cmd., 6524: Lord Houghton's Minority Report.

74 *The Times*, 5 February 1970.

75 Lord Redcliffe-Maud quoted in *The Times*, 17 June 1970.

76 *Ibid.*

77 Margaret Thatcher Foundation: *Conservative Party Manifesto*, 11 April 1979, www.margaretthatcher.org, visited on 4 April 2011.

78 *Standards of Conduct in Public Life* (1995), Cmd., 2850-II. Transcripts of Evidence: Ivor Crewe, para. 16, p. 6.

79 *Ibid.*, David Rendell MP, para. 43, p. 14.

80 *Standards of Conduct in Public Life* (1995), Cmd., 3702-I.

81 *Ibid.*, para. 13, p. 4.

82 Martin Bell, *A Very British Revolution: The Expenses Scandal and How to Save Our Democracy* (London: Icon Books, 2009), p. 28.

2   Decline and fall of the civic tradition and civil society

> What man loses by the social contract are his natural liberty and the absolute right
> to anything that tempts and that he can take. What he gains by the social contract
> is civil liberty ... which is limited by the general will.
>
> Jean-Jacques Rousseau, *The Social Contract* (1762)[1]

In 1935, the Bishop of Manchester wrote to his clergy requesting that they
remember, in their church services on Sunday 5 May, the centenary of the passing of the Municipal Corporations Act of 1835. He suggested that the Act
'marked the beginning of a revolution in our civic life'.[2] Local government and
municipal corporations stood at the apogee of their status and esteem. The
Bishop was not alone in wishing to acknowledge the passing of the Act. The
National Association of Local Government Officers (NALGO) held numerous
celebrations and indeed commissioned a weighty volume, *A Century of Progress*,
to commemorate the Act. Its editors – Harold Laski, William Robson and Ivor
Jennings – extolled the virtues of local government trumpeting the contribution of municipal government to 'progress' and citing the successes of town
government especially in public health. Reductions in death rates and the
elimination of cholera which could now be regarded as 'something remote and
oriental' and the reduction in the incidence of such diseases as tuberculosis
were considered to be 'utopian' achievements. Additionally, Laski made tribute
to the members of NALGO claiming that 'such a corporate spirit prevails
among local government officers' that there was indeed a 'great future [for]
English local government'.[3] William Robson, the academic jurist and reformer
from the LSE, had also been commissioned to write a series of articles for *The
Times* to commemorate the passing of the Act. There was no reticence in his
praise for local government: 'the value of our local government system cannot
in the last resort be fully appreciated except in terms of the civic effort from
which the several services have sprung and which is their unifying link. The

greatest conquest of all is the defeat of apathy and indifference by a growing sense of civic pride'.[4] This kind of eulogy was echoed elsewhere: Alderman Modley, the Deputy Mayor of Plymouth, addressed the local Foresters Friendly Society in 1940 and claimed that there had never been any corruption in Plymouth and that the 'Corporation had enriched the life of the citizens'. The toastmaster on behalf of the Foresters hailed the Corporation and urged that the councillors should 'set themselves the task of attaining a high standard of morality based on righteousness and sobriety and [be] free from any taint of corruption'.[5] What are the implications of this kind of thinking, and particularly why is civic effort important when trying to understand and explain the incidence of corruption in public and political life? By civic tradition, we mean the institutions of municipal and local government. The vibrancy and effectiveness of civic tradition however is also dependent on a strong and active civil society of clubs, societies and voluntary associations that can act both as pressure groups and also hold local government to account.

At the risk of constructing an elliptical argument, the presence of a strong civil society is a powerful inhibitor of the incidence of corruption. This is not to say that corruption does not occur where there is apparently a strong civil society. However, the converse of this proposition is more likely to be true: where civil society is weak the incidence of corruption is likely to be greater. Strong civil societies are characterised by a citizenry involved through voluntary effort within the public domain, and this provides a strong ethical base for the conduct of public life. A strong civil community is marked by an active, organised public-spirited citizenry and by egalitarian political relations sustained by a social fabric of trust and co-operation.[6] Moreover, organised and cohesive groups that can act in watchdog or advocacy roles can often achieve change or some accountability of office holders. Where there are strong social networks as well as a strong associational life, the prospects for civil society are good and the deterrence of corruption becomes possible. On the other hand, civil society can disintegrate if it is captured by interest groups who seek to expand the role of the state via subsidies, grants and other special arrangements for their client groups.[7] What is more likely, however, is where social life is fragmented, where there is social isolation and a culture of distrust, then the prospects for corruption are greater.

Citizenship within a civil community requires active participation in public affairs and the pursuit of public good over and above individual or private ends. Those that do participate in public life as elected office holders in these circumstances can pursue a civic virtue that is altruistic and enlightened which can also produce many shared benefits. By contrast, the absence of a strong civil society produces circumstances where the maximising of material gain and the securing of short-run advantage have primacy over all other considerations. In the most extreme situations, it can result in an 'amoral familism'[8] where the institution of the family is more powerful than any other, and some historians have argued that such conditions have been critical in Italian society since its political system has become 'blocked' and 'deeply degenerate' producing by the 1980s a 'new and organised rapacity on the part of politicians [and] a spoils system which extended throughout the peninsula'.[9] The reasons for such a blocked political system stem from the constitution of the Italian Republic with its numerous checks and balances and the tensions between the central state, the regions and the cities. The conditions of stasis can only be overcome, apparently, by bribery and corruption which come to be regarded as suitable tools just to get things done. Further, because of the culture of 'amoral familism', civil society is too weak to counter corruption amongst politicians. Indeed, at its most extreme, several Italian cities – Naples and Palermo particularly – became notable for corruption with collusion between politicians and organised crime. By contrast, it is often assumed that Britain is a strong civil society. Such a view is often articulated by politicians, especially when they apprehend corruption in other societies and states, but perhaps we should express caution here: the development of a strong civil society is a long and evolutionary process but neither is it irreversible.[10]

It may well be that the general increase in affluence in the 1950s and 1960s contributed to the development of a more 'family centred individualism'[11] which worked against the sustenance of a strong civil society. The articulation of the Seven Principles of Public Life – selflessness, integrity, objectivity, accountability, openness, honesty and leadership – by the Nolan Committee in 1995 is perhaps then almost a counter-intuitive expression of the weakness of civil society in late twentieth-century Britain and perhaps an attempt to recover a more traditional form of virtue ethics.[12] Thus, although Britain has both strong civic and civil traditions, perhaps we need to consider whether over the period 1929–94 the strength of those traditions has wilted or at least the energies and efforts that had sustained their relevance in the arena of local government were transferred elsewhere. In fact, voluntary commitment to other causes – such as animal welfare, heritage and consumer protection – would seem to have grown at the expense of local activism that focused on urban government in particular. That long-standing voluntary association – the Women's Institute – had launched the 'Keep Britain Tidy' campaign although its original impetus emanated from a fear of litter encroaching upon the countryside. However, it would be legitimate to argue that these 'do good' organisations were unlikely in themselves to check corruption. Britain has enjoyed a strong voluntary tradition and that tradition seemed in excellent health in the 1950s and 1960s. For example, membership of the National Trust doubled in the 1950s and doubled again in the 1960s. The membership of the Royal Society for the Protection of Birds also doubled in the 1950s. The Consumer Association was founded in 1957, and within two years, it had 140,000 members.[13] Significantly, more traditional forms of political activism – leafleting and canvassing during elections – undoubtedly declined. National party leaderships also resolved to direct and fund election campaigns. Understandable as such a strategy might have been, it had the effect of undermining the party activists' 'moral claim' to influence party policy.[14] Political pressure groups, such as the Campaign for Nuclear Disarmament, could often owe no allegiance to political parties. Thus, in many respects, civil society, as suggested by the nature of voluntarism which focused on consumer interests, rural issues and heritage, conservation and charity, was steered away from local government and the city in particular. Consequently, public attitudes towards local government became marked increasingly by indifference. In fact, the capacity of civil society to act as a check upon politicians' potential for misconduct and corruption is not infinite. More likely perhaps has been a lack of time or enthusiasm to become involved in community and town politics. In the new towns, for example, where the planners' hopes of 'a vibrant community life, with abundant volunteer residents gathering in tenants' common rooms foundered on lack of leisure among the numerous young families who came predominantly from the skilled working class'.[15]

It is contended here that the virtues of the civic tradition had reached their apogee by the 1930s and that they may have also received a temporary boost during the Attlee government of 1945–51, but thereafter they began to erode.[16] Additionally, the capacity of civil society to hold local government to account also diminished as its energies became centred elsewhere. The virtues of local government that were articulated by theorists such as Laski had a long pedigree and were derived from a classical education producing 'an unquestioned adoption of classical antiquity as a reference point for the present'.[17] They drew on what were thought to be the virtues of the English: 'a capacity to govern others and control themselves, [an] aptitude for combining freedom with order, their public spirit, their vigour and manliness of character, their strong but not slavish respect for public opinion'.[18] This summary by the Clarendon Commissioners of the virtues instilled by the Nine Great Public Schools as the 'nurseries of our statesmen' in 1864 might also be applied to local councillors and aldermen. Indeed, Lord Snell, who had been chairman of the LCC in 1934–37 argued that although an average town councillor may not have a 'conscious theory of the state, and no knowledge of the civic idealism of ancient Greece; [but] he could, like them, ... fall in love with the city in which he dwells and be sustained by an ideal ... in devoting himself to his native city and spending himself in her service'. Snell's affinity with the Clarendon Commissioners was demonstrated further when he said local government 'has been a precious nursery of civic virtues, the fruitful training ground for the national and imperial service; and it has helped to produce a reserve of administrative capacity on which British civilisation may continue to draw'.[19] The city had solved the questions of public health, public works and public services such as transport, gas and electricity. Now it would promote culture, learning and the arts. This heady idealism also had another motive: to promote active citizenship which would serve as an antidote to totalitarian dictatorships which were emerging as malignant shadows across continental Europe. For Laski, Robson and Graham Wallas, the city and civilisation were coterminous from which the foundations of freedom could be laid enabling civil society to flourish. There would be no room for corruption in a civilisation marked by the characteristics of British liberalism freedom, order and progress.[20]

These ideals also had practical political application through Fabianism of which Sidney and Beatrice Webb were the principal architects. Their histories and analyses of the traditions of English local government drew on deep-rooted traditions going back to the parish, vestry and ancient corporations. Their thinking was extended by Graham Wallas who had become the chairman of the Fabian Parliamentary League in 1887 and later of its successor, the Political Committee of the Fabian Society. He strived to promote co-operation between socialists and progressive Liberals. Wallas had extolled the ideal of the Athenian *polis* where an educated citizenry conducted civilised and informed debate to make considered decisions for their community. It was this thinking that caused him to oppose the 1902 Conservative Education Act believing that the school boards were perfect examples of the principle of local democratic control of education. Although he broke with the Webbs after 1904 and veered towards the progressive New Liberalism and writing for *The Nation*, his thinking remained influential. In particular, the practical, virtuous and free from theory application of such lessons was carried out by Ernest Simon, a Manchester industrialist, who also had a formative relationship with the Webbs. Simon was not a rigid party politician, and like Wallas he migrated from one position to another. Initially a Liberal, he subsequently joined the Labour Party, which he saw as an instrument for progressive reform. He had first been elected to Manchester City Council in 1912, and his involvement in housing reform is already well known, but he became increasingly convinced that the survival of local democracy was dependent on the education of the citizenry; and with Eva Hubback, secretary of the National Union of Societies for Equal Citizenship and principal of Morley College for Adult Education in Lambeth, Simon established the Council for Education for Citizenship in 1931.[21] This would seem to be a practical expression of the Athenian ideal of the *polis*. Civil society by the 1930s then was characterised by voluntary effort, and in the arena of local government, it was imbued with a lofty idealism, at least in the minds of its leading advocates.[22] Herbert Morrison, too, leaned in this direction[23] even though he was also known as a pragmatist and a machine politician of the type that Lord Jessel, the President of the National Union of Ratepayers' Associations, would have loathed. Morrison exuded an almost puritanical zeal in his advocacy of clean local government. In his *How London Is Governed* (1949), he gave sage advice to Labour councillors warning them not to fraternise with paid officials and not to accept publicly funded hospitality so that they could be 'free of the least suspicion of personal interest in making appointments or promotions'.[24] He was also able to give a populist colour to this approach when he told the *Daily Mail* in 1935: 'the only thing for which I would preserve capital punishment would be jobbery, bribery and corruption in public services or robbery from public funds'.[25] Nevertheless, the confidence that the national elite was prepared to invest in local government was signified by the Local Government Act 1929 which extended the responsibilities of local government with the abolition of the Poor Law Guardians, the rating responsibilities of which had already been transferred to county, borough and district councils by the Rating and Valuation Act of 1925. The press was fulsome in its praise for Neville Chamberlain who had steered the Local Government Bill through parliament. Indeed, the passage of the Bill championed by a member of the Chamberlain political dynasty was living testimony of the tradition of civic pride working in harmony with the central state. It represented a high point of confidence in the competence and efficiency of local government. The authors of the legislation were in fact Sidney and Beatrice Webb. George Lansbury was especially enthusiastic claiming that the country owed special thanks to the 'genius' of Webb and 'his brilliant wife'. He caught the mood of the time: 'I think that the unselfish work that these two public spirited people have done merits some word of congratulations from this House'.[26] The tradition of permissiveness in British government policy in the nineteenth century had fostered local enthusiasm allowing local government to expand its range of responsibilities and services – street lighting, police, sanitary management and libraries – and these had now been extended by central government fiat to include education, public assistance, welfare, public health, housing, slum clearance, roads as well as town and country planning. It was indeed a remarkable range of responsibilities probably greater and more varied than in any other European country.

The idealism expressed through Laski's and Robson's prose and the praise heaped on the Webbs at the passing of the Act in 1929 was not of course the whole story. It should be remembered that *A Century of Progress* was in fact a political riposte to the recommendations of the May Committee (1931) and the Ray Committee (1932) which sought to constrain local government. The financial crisis of the summer of 1931 had seen the collapse of the Labour government and the establishment of a National Coalition headed by Ramsay MacDonald. Budgetary discipline had seen a return of classical economic thinking demanding budget savings. The May Committee recommended £96 million of savings in public expenditure. The recommendations of both May and Ray hit hard at local government. Sir William Ray, the Conservative leader of the LCC, sought radical solutions, and his committee recommended the abolition of local government control of public housing and the end of the system of subsidies for council house building. Further, Ray criticised local government administration of outdoor relief.[27] This was no doubt a political swipe at Poplarism and the expenditure on poor relief by a number of Labour-controlled

London boroughs. The London Borough of Poplar had defied LCC regulations on poor relief expenditure in 1921, and it had become a great *cause célèbre* for the political left throughout the interwar years.

The recommendations of the Ray Committee gave impetus to the growing ratepayer movement, which represented a more traditional view of the purpose of public expenditure. Thus, Lord Jessel, one of the most informed members of the House of Lords on matters of local government, issued a memorandum in April 1935 on the forthcoming municipal elections lamenting the lack of interest in local affairs. He had spoken vigorously against the Local Government Act of 1929 on the grounds that it reduced local government borrowing powers and consequently local autonomy.[28] Local authorities had vast expenditures, and there was a danger that Labour Party victories in these forthcoming elections would, he claimed, result in the 'subordination of civic interests to Socialist Party tactics'. He went on to lambast the inefficiency of local government administration in Labour-controlled towns and cities suggesting that they had used poor relief payments to bribe the electorate. This was an important argument since it associated the Labour Party with, potentially, a form of clientism and even corrupt behaviour as it had entailed the payment of poor relief at rates above the scales approved by the Ministry of Health. More generally, Poplarism was used to denote any defiance of central government by Labour councils especially on matters of poor relief expenditure. Additionally, Jessel complained that the LCC had prohibited the customary celebration of Empire Day in London's schools.[29] Jessel was also supported by the likes of Sir Waldron Smithers, the Conservative MP for Chislehurst in Kent. Smithers, speaking at the Ratepayers Protection League conference in Brighton, linked high spending and high rates with a high incidence of corruption claiming that there were 'hundreds' of cases of 'nepotism and corruption' particularly in Labour-controlled towns and cities.[30] He spoke out in the interests of 'clean government'. Similar sentiments were expressed by Hubert Carr-Gomm, the MP for Rotherhithe, so much so that he advocated the introduction of proportional representation as a means of securing the presence of minority opinion to counter the great sway which Labour was beginning to exert in the London boroughs.[31] This was an unusual proposal in the circumstances since such a provision had been attempted by the British government in 1920 in its Government of Ireland Act to accommodate minority Catholic opinion in Ulster. However, the Northern Ireland Parliament moved quickly and abolished proportional representation for local government elections in 1922. There was in fact considerable variability across the kingdom with elections in some localities marked by 'apathy', and elsewhere they were subject to 'keen contests'.[32] Nonetheless, there were distinct regional patterns. In South Wales, for example, the strength of Labour was such that many potential voters were paralysed by the 'futility of any effective opposition to the Socialist machine'.[33] In some districts, it was alleged that 'businessmen and property owners hesitate to set themselves up against the champions of the rate spenders and opposition to them maybe attended by inconvenient results'.[34] These views were echoed by the chairman of the Council for the Preservation of Rural Wales, Clough Williams-Ellis. Speaking in Dorking in 1931, he had, after a tour of English towns, become a 'wiser and sadder man', and he had concluded that 'municipal affairs were generally conducted with incompetence [and] corruption'. This was not 'straight graft on a cash basis after the Chicago model but less frank arrangements and concessions among the city governors and officials – favouritism, nepotism, log-rolling [American slang associated with corrupt railway investments], commission-hunting and the frequent sacrifice of the public good to private profit'.[35] In some respects, the sentiments expressed by Laski and Robson on the one hand and Lord Jessel on the other were familiar. The former were rooted in the traditions of nineteenth-century liberal 'improvers', and the latter derived his rationale from the so-called 'economists'. However, the patterns of electoral behaviour were beginning to produce the conditions which were conducive to the creation of party fiefdoms. For example, in County Durham, which was a Labour stronghold where Labour possessed eighty council seats in 1934 whilst commanding 105,000 votes compared with the Liberals and Independents who held only nineteen council seats on the strength of 73,000 votes.[36] In Glamorgan in the 1937 local elections, forty-one out of sixty-six vacancies were returned to unopposed candidates of whom twenty-seven were Labour Party members. The contrast between Laski's and Robson's idealism about the value of local government and Jessel's complaints were obviously inspired by different political beliefs, but their disagreement also signified something else about the position of local government in the mid-1930s: the apparent integrity of local government was already being brought into doubt. Perhaps not surprisingly then attempts to promote greater rectitude and probity in local government came from the political right rather than the left.

The arguments of the leading members of the Prevention of Corruption League, such as Lord Crewe who had been Minister for War in the 1931 coalition, may seem now abstruse and arcane, but the members of the League regarded themselves as influential. The League also had the support of the Indian Empire Society, a meeting of which held in the Albert Hall and addressed by Winston Churchill, illustrated the importance of the India factor in perceptions of corruption and by implication the virtue of Britain's local self-government. Conservative opposition to Indian independence and indeed generally constitutional reform in India was couched in terms of the danger of the growth of corruption. Thus, Churchill claimed that Gandhi was surrounded by a coterie of Bombay millionaires whose intent would result in 'nepotism, back-scratching, graft and corruption'.[37] The Indian Empire Society also gave evidence to the Joint Select Committee on Indian Constitutional Reform asserting that corruption in India was widespread.[38]

The views of the members of Prevention of Corruption League were not then unusual and served to sustain the pre-eminence of the British self-image that it had devised institutions and cultivated a public service ethic that if not immune to the dangers of corruption was sufficiently well fortified to maintain a robust defence. In many respects, then, the League was a perfect example of a civil society organisation that challenged the ascendancy of the political party machines.

Despite Laski's and Robson's eulogies and despite the patriotic assertions of the Prevention of Corruption League, the independence of local government in Britain was being eroded. Its functions and range were being adjusted by central government against a backdrop of economic and financial uncertainty. In the first instance, the role of local government was being reshaped by central government. The Local Government Act 1929 had abolished the 635 Poor Law Unions, and the matter of poor relief was to be dealt with by public assistance committees under the control of county councils, county boroughs and municipal boroughs. Further, a system of derating was introduced to relieve pressure on business, and the lost income was replaced by 'block grants' from central government. This re-enforced an existing trend since grants-in-aid of the rates had expanded from 1834 onwards so that the treasury funded the transport of criminals from gaol to embarkation in the case of passage to the colonies. In 1849, the treasury took on the funding of teachers in Poor Law schools. It was Goschen's budget of 1887 that had been so critical in reforming the 'financial relations between central and local government'.[39] Further, the Local Government Act (1888) provided for the reform of local government finance as the Bank of England established a local taxation account into which revenues from excise duties and probate duties were paid. Thus, by the 1890s, some local authorities were already receiving more than 60 per cent of their income from the Exchequer, and the trend towards ever more central funding – admittedly to secure an equalisation in the allocation of resources for social purposes – had the effect of reducing the autonomy of local councils. So paradoxically, the 1929 Act increased local government responsibilities via the adoption of poor law responsibilities, but other measures reduced its responsibilities. The establishment of the Central Electricity Board in 1926 was the signal for the beginning of the national grid which could distribute electricity at a cost far lower than a municipal authority. Electricity and gas had been, initially, municipal services, but as technology improved, so the scale of capital investment far outstripped the capabilities of local government institutions. Additionally, the creation of the National Health Service after 1945 subsumed many locally managed hospitals. Later still the Water Act (1963) set up a National Water Resources Board, and a national plan for water was published in 1973; and changes in the management of education between 1983 and 1987 all served to reduce local autonomy, making local government a subcontractor of central government administration and a conduit through which to pass funds shaped by central government priorities. This trend, working over a long period c. 1929–c. 1987, had the effect of reducing local autonomy and dissipating the ethic of civic virtue which had reached its confident maturation in the 1930s and was exemplified by Manchester, Birmingham and the LCC. Thereafter, there was a significant diminution of the vitality of local civil society, producing fiefdoms under the control of one particular party, creating the conditions of apathy and the feeling that there was no way around the local party machine. It helped to create the conditions where local party organisations and indeed whole local authorities could be captured by politicians who were prepared to abandon the gentlemanly politics handed down in the Victorian civic gospel. It was in these circumstances that corruption could flourish.[40] The growth of corruption, particularly as exemplified by the cases of John Poulson, T. Dan Smith and Sidney Sporle, undermined the status of local government decisively. Government ministers had lost confidence in the efficacy of local government, and between 1982 and 1984, the Secretary of State acquired powers to withhold funds from what were considered profligate councils and ultimately to deny local authority autonomy by the device of 'rate capping' which was used to punish political opposition as much as anything else. Additionally, the Greater London Council (GLC) was abolished in 1986. The long history of independent local authorities was finally brought to a close with the introduction of the community charge or 'poll tax' as it was named infamously. For many, local government had seemed to lose all legitimacy, and in so doing, opportunities for corruption increased with Dame Shirley Porter's notorious gerrymandering in Westminster City Council, Derek Hatton's capture of Liverpool by the tactics of 'entryism' in the 1980s and the 'junkets for votes' scandal in Glasgow in the 1990s. The Labour Party's National Executive Committee was forced to take disciplinary action against the Militant Tendency in Liverpool amidst claims of 'intimidation and corruption'[41] and against Labour's local leadership, Pat Lally and Alex Mosson, in Glasgow[42].

The vitality of local government as articulated through the civic tradition espoused by Laski, Wallas, Snell and also Morrison had reached its apogee in the 1930s but was gradually eroded as the central state became increasingly interventionist and also by how it controlled local government finance through grants-in-aid of the rates.[43] That vitality was also undermined by societal changes that diluted the vigour of civil society – voluntary organisations, clubs, societies and pressure groups – which had previously acted as watchdog holding local government to account and creating a vibrant urban political culture. Civil society had thus become increasingly disconnected from local government. In part, this was a product of demography and suburbanisation. After 1951, inner-city populations shrank markedly. Social and political leaders with middle-class backgrounds had also withdrawn from local political life. This trend had already been in train before 1939 and now accelerated after 1950.

The motor car made it possible for those that could afford it to distance themselves from the negative externalities of urban life:

> Larger shops, remote and more centralized firms and privatised travel eroded neigh-
> bourliness and a sense of place. Lighting became utilitarian, unsightly traffic signs
> proliferated, and fewer citizens felt the pride in community which had led their pred-
> ecessors so generously to fund urban amenities. The religious motive and the sense of
> stewardship of wealth that had nourished the 'civic gospel' idea were waning ....[44]

The sense of community that had sustained Victorian pride in city centres
was critically at risk. Even Birmingham's council levelled the city centre that
had 'epitomized Victorian city pride'.[45] These developments and their effects are
sometimes hard to trace, but the break-up of communities as well as the increasing privatisation of leisure denied nourishment to the conditions which had
allowed civil society directed at civic ends to be sustained. Civil society is reliant upon trust and social capital. For many, the post-war period has become
characterised by a growing apathy as far as the electorate is concerned in respect
of local government. Turnouts were often low, and it was claimed that votes
were cast either as affirmations or protests at the performance of the national
government. For many voting was essentially a declaration of belonging or loyalty to a class, ethnic group and party which was not informed by performance
or policy matters. In London, turnout for GLC elections declined from 43.8 per
cent in 1964 to 36 per cent in 1973. In London boroughs, electoral turnout
hovered between 35.7 per cent and 38.4 per cent between 1964 and 1974. It
rose above 40 per cent in the late 1970s and the 1980s but fell back again to 34.7
per cent by 1998. For the rest of England and Wales, the turnout in local elections declined in the metropolitan boroughs from 39.1 per cent in 1973 to 25.2
per cent in 1998. Admittedly, there were many fluctuations and a significant
high point in 1990. Perhaps of greater importance though was that the combination of low turnout combined with a stable command of the total number of
council seats across all metropolitan boroughs revealed a remarkable monopoly
of power by the Labour Party: between 1976 and 1995, Labour's share of all
council seats never fell below 43.9 per cent and reached a maximum 81 per cent
of all available seats in 1995.[46] The existence of such Labour fiefdoms and weak
oppositions has been perceived by many to be a source of corrupt behaviour[47]. It
could be claimed that this was nothing new but its effect was to make local
government insular and remote from the lives of the citizens. Indeed, there had
been attempts to open up council meetings. As early as 1908, Arthur Henderson
had promoted a private member's bill resulting in the Local Authorities
(Admission of the Press) Act with the specific purpose of enabling the public to
be informed about the activities of their local government. This is only part of
the story. What is contended here is that changes in social and economic conditions and changes in the urban fabric had deleterious effects on the dynamism
of wider civil society. When de Tocqueville visited America in 1831, he was
struck by what he called the 'habits of the heart' which were favourable

to maintenance of democratic, accountable institutions.[48] He thought that a society's propensity to form civil and political organisations had special consequences for the members and participants in those organisations who develop loyalty and adherence to the rules of the organisations. More recently, Robert Putnam and also Francis Fukuyama have addressed this matter.[49] For both of these theorists, active participation in public life and strong civil society is characterised by a public-spirited citizenry and by a social fabric of trust and co-operation. Putnam's studies of Italy suggest that in regions where civil society and civic tradition are weak, such as in southern Calabria, the 'ancient plague of political corruption' is all too apparent.[50] His survey work suggests that there was an overall sense of powerlessness, citizens were more likely to regard politicians as dishonest and there was a greater fear of lawlessness. Moreover, the only way round this was to cheat oneself, to break traffic rules, to avoid taxation and to cheat the welfare system. Cheating was so pervasive that not to cheat was regarded by many as naïve. For Fukuyama, these are the traits of a low-trust society, and in these conditions, corruption is always a risk.

In the regions of the United Kingdom, there are certainly echoes of this pattern, and the cities of Belfast, Glasgow and Newcastle display such characteristics. More generally, the Salmon Commission certainly identified the condition of powerlessness amongst the citizenry. We also need to recognise that local government and urban society were also part of a wider social and cultural context which requires consideration of whether changes in standards of behaviour and conduct exhibited a new kind of laxity or permissiveness. The 1950s and 1960s witnessed growing anxiety about public and private morality. Some historians have asserted that there was a greater permissiveness than anything hitherto and that liberalisation at this moment marked a revolution in lifestyles and personal freedoms and therefore that these two decades were a time of outstanding historical significance.[51] So was the incidence of corruption in public life and politics part of that permissiveness? The legacy of Victorian attitudes concerning the moral rectitude of public men persisted at least into the 1950s. It is difficult however to plot key moments in the process of moral and ethical change, but such a narrative might include John Belcher in1948, a Minister at the Board of Trade, duped by Sidney Stanley, a streetwise spiv. Stanley claimed to act as contact man, in fact a kind of lobbyist, who could fix things with ministers. He was a charlatan, but Belcher fell on his sword and resigned exhibiting the honourable behaviour of the time; but by 1962, John Profumo's behaviour was regarded as dishonourable not because of his sexual dalliance with Christine Keeler but because he had lied to the House of Commons. For those who like turning points, the Profumo case fits the bill. By 1972, the behaviour of John Poulson was seen as venal and representative of a new ruthless business entrepreneur and for some the 'unpleasant and unacceptable face of capitalism',[52] whereas Lords Jellicoe and Lambton in 1973 were perceived in more traditional terms as effete and indulgent aristocrats. Such a linear decline from honourable resignation to naked venality suggested a breakdown in traditional morality. The problem with the study of corruption is that there can be brief periods of apparent probity and virtue suddenly sabotaged by a scandalous corruption case.[53] Thus, we might see the Northcote–Trevelyan reforms in the 1850s as signifying a new equilibrium in matters of public probity in the civil service, but even here there were transgressions as the investigations in the Admiralty in respect of dockyard expenditure revealed in 1860.[54] Again the brief period between the passing of the Local Government Act in 1929 and the eruption of the Glasgow scandal in 1933 might be similarly regarded. Further, even in the period of Attlee's apparent Cromwellian puritanism, the Belcher case intruded.

Arguably, corruption has been ever present, but it has often been obscured by the hegemony of, essentially, liberal ideas such as the notion of selfless public service, the honest stewardship of the public purse and the imperial mission to export good government to other peoples around the globe. The reality of local government and particularly government in the major towns and cities was that it seemed to have increasingly less relevance to those who voted in local elections. This was reflected in the decline in electoral turnout as already illustrated. It was also apparent from the withdrawal of industrial and merchant elites from city government. This was especially marked in cities such as Glasgow, Birmingham, Manchester and Newcastle. The combination of the withdrawal of the traditional elite from city affairs had a number of very specific consequences. In the first instance, the older elite was replaced by a new political class recruited from the trade unions, small businessmen and some professionals and those who had time to devote to public affairs such as the retired and very often married women who were not in paid employment. Further, the increasingly technical nature of finance, planning and education policy saw an ascendancy of the paid officers over the elected councillors. In some respects, it would be possible to assert that the calibre and quality of elected councillors declined. Thus, Dame Evelyn Sharp, Permanent Secretary, addressed the annual conference of the Association of Municipal Corporations in 1960 and lamented that men and women of sufficient ability did not come forward: 'finding councillors of sufficient calibre to make use of the [local] authorities' potentialities' had been apparent in the problems experienced in Birmingham and many other cities.[55] It was quite possible that this problem of apparent lack of ability was a function of the party machines. The selection of candidates by local party organisations was often a cursory affair. Selection panels were concerned that prospective candidates had sufficient time to devote to municipal affairs. Local Labour organisations often concluded agreements with local trade unions, and in some places – Glasgow, Newcastle and Doncaster – particular electoral wards were considered to be in the gift of a particular union or the local trades council, and so bargains were struck to place a trade union candidate in a safe ward.[56] Combined with low turnout and uncontested wards, this was a system of placemen reliant on the patronage of the party machine but little different from the eighteenth-century

MPs dependent on the favour of the Duke of Newcastle or some other political magnate. Finally, the emergence of the new breed of 'career politician' promoted a new social ideal type who devoted his or her life exclusively to politics and nothing else or at least chose other employment as a convenience to sustain a political career. In some senses, the term 'career politician' has a pejorative quality suggesting that entry into politics signified a career 'on the make'. Caution is important here as disinterestedness, probity and the other public virtues are as common amongst politicians as they are amongst those employed in public service. Indeed, the relations between politicians – national, local, career or volunteer committed to the ideals of public service – and the ethics of society are subtle and complex. Nevertheless, politicians and all members of the political classes whether national or local can become enclosed in a private world marked by a private language and increasingly private political quarrels. Indeed, in the Westminster gerrymandering scandal, the four most prominent perpetrators of the corruption display a variety of social types: the leader of the council, Dame Shirley Porter, who was the Tesco heiress with immense personal wealth whose drive and ambitions led her to extraordinary judgements indicative of a closed world of personal battles; David Weeks, university-educated and single-minded party hatchet man; Barry Legg who despite the scandal became Conservative MP for Milton Keynes South-West in 1992; and Doctor Michael Dutt who had been unsuccessful as a Conservative MEP candidate in Strathclyde East and also as a parliamentary candidate for Leicester South. These profiles illustrate perhaps that it is difficult to attribute general social or cultural causes to corrupt behaviour and misconduct but rather corruption and misconduct is perhaps a facet of behaviour in what politicians themselves call a 'rough trade'.

The Porter case was indeed extraordinary and almost defies generalisation. However, the longer-run theme that local government lost autonomy and independence and was regarded with indifference by local populations as simply another manifestation of the central state bureaucracy holds good. The local authority may provide all manner of social goods – education, housing and care services – with varying degrees of efficiency. Should it fail the consequence is rarely electoral defeat of the ruling party, since although they are services collectively provided they are individually consumed. For the most part, then the potential for corruption in local government more likely arises from circumstances where civic traditions and civic pride have been ground down. The sources of this decline have evidently been benign – to distribute social and public goods and services on an equitable basis – but with the result that local government has been marginalised in the popular consciousness. Low electoral turnout, uncontested wards, candidates subservient to the wishes of the party machines, a decline in the quality and ability of elected councillors and the rise of career politicians who regard a stint in local politics as a rite of passage produce the conditions of isolation and separateness which in turn reduce accountability. Such circumstances can produce a culture where corruption can take root. Further, if local society is not organised into cohesive groups that make for a vibrant civil society, then corruption becomes possible unless it is exposed by the press, discovered by auditors or used by politicians themselves as part of a reform platform. It is reckoned that Britain has a strong civil society and indeed it does but its energy became increasingly less focused on local urban government. This coupled with rapid change helps to produce the conditions where corruption can flourish.

Notes

1 Rousseau, *Social Contract* (2004), p. 32.
2 *The Times*, 28 March 1935.
3 Laski, H., W.I. Jennings, E. Halevy, Sir I. Jennings and W.A. Robson, *A Century of Municipal Progress* (London: Allen and Unwin, 1935).
4 *The Times*, 10 December 1935.
5 *Western Morning News*, 26 February 1940.
6 Whitely, P., *Political Participation in Britain: The Decline and Revival of Civic Culture* (Basingstoke: Palgrave Macmillan, 2011).
7 There is an extensive literature on this subject but for a useful introduction (see Fukuyama, *State Building* (2004)).
8 Banfield, *Moral Basis* (1958).
9 Ginsborg, *Italy and Its Discontents* (2001), pp. 179–81.
10 Stoneman, P., *This Thing Called Trust: Civic Society in Britain* (Basingstoke: Palgrave Macmillan, 2008).
11 Hirst in Tiratsoo, N., *From Blitz to Blair* (London: Phoenix, 1997).
12 Grayling, *Ideas That Matter* (2009), p. 529.
13 Harrison, *Seeking* (2009), pp. 132–6.
14 *Ibid.*, p. 466.
15 *Ibid.*, p. 155.
16 Doyle, B., 'The changing functions of urban government', in Daunton, M. (ed.), *The Cambridge Urban History of Britain*, vol. III, 1840–1950 (Cambridge: Cambridge University Press, 2000), pp. 312–13.
17 Young, K., 'Re-reading the municipal progress: a crisis re-visited', in Loughlin, M. (ed.), *Half a Century of Municipal Decline: 1935–1985* (London: Allen and Unwin, 1985), p. 20.
18 *The Clarendon Report* 1864 in Maclure, J., *Educational Documents: England and Wales 1816–1967* (London: Methuen, 1965), pp. 87–8.
19 Lord Snell in Laski et al., *A Century of Progress*, p. 81.
20 Joyce, P., *The Rule of Freedom: Liberalism and the Modern City* (London: Verso, 2003).
21 Simon, E. *Training for Citizenship* (London: Oxford University Press, 1935).
22 There was an extensive literature on this subject. Laski was the most notable figure, but there were many others: Peddie, J.R., *The British Citizen: A Book for Young Readers* (London: General Books LLC, 1920); Masterman, C.F.G., *How England is Governed* (London: Selwyn and Blount, 1921); Simon, E., *A City Council from Within* (London: Longmans Green, 1926).
23 Morrison, H., *How London Is Governed* (London: People's University Press, 1949).
24 Quoted in Donoghue, B. and G.W. Jones, *Herbert Morrison: Portrait of a Politician* (London: Weidenfeld and Nicolson, 1973), p. 197.
25 *Daily Mail*, 19 July 1935 quoted in Donoughue and Jones, *Herbert Morrison*, p. 197.
26 *Hansard*, HC Debates, 28 November 1928, vol. 223, cc. 477–562.

27 Young, K., 'Re-reading municipal progress'.

28 *Hansard*, House of Lords Debates, 29 June 1932, vol. 85, cc. 294–352.

29 Lord Jessel in *The Times*, 18 October 1935.

30 *Hull Daily Mail*, 18 October 1938.

31 Hubert Carr-Gomm in *The Times*, 10 January 1936.

32 *The Times*, 2 April 1935.

33 *The Times*, 23 February 1937.

34 *Ibid*.

35 *The Times*, 2 February 1931.

36 *The Times*, 22 February 1937.

37 *The Times*, 19 March 1931.

38 *The Times*, 11 October 1933.

39 Baugh, G.C., 'Government grants in aid of the rates', *Historical Research*, 65 (1992), pp. 215–33. See also Davis, J. 'Central government and the towns', in Daunton (2000), p. 272.

40 Smith, T.D., *Dan Smith: An Autobiography* (Newcastle: Oriel Press, 1970); Milne, E., *No Shining Armour* (London: John Calder, 1976), *Royal Commission on Standards of Conduct in Public Life* (1976), Cmnd., 6524, para. 8, p. 119.

41 *The Times*, 29 January 1986.

42 *The Guardian*, 27 October 1997.

43 Baugh, 'Government grants', pp. 215–32.

44 Harrison, *Seeking*, p. 147.

45 Harrison, B., *Finding a Role? The United Kingdom 1970–1990* (Oxford: Oxford University Press, 2010), p. 77.

46 Rallings, C. and M. Thrasher (eds.), *Local Elections in Britain: A Statistical Digest* (Plymouth: Local Government Chronicle Elections Centre, 2003), pp. vii–xv.

47 *Royal Commission on Standards of Conduct in Public Life* (1976), minority report of Audrey Ward Jackson.

48 Tocqueville, *Democracy in America* (1994), p. 299.

49 Putnam, et al., *Making Democracy Work*; and Fukuyama, *Trust* (1995).

50 Putnam, et al., *Making Democracy Work*, pp. 111–12.

51 Marwick, A., *The Sixties: Cultural Revolution in Britain, France, Italy and the U.S. c. 1958–1974* (Oxford: Oxford University Press, 1998). See also Donnelly, M., *Sixties Britain: Culture, Society and Politics* (Harlow: Pearson Longman, 2005); Jarvis, M., *Conservative Governments: Morality and Social Change in Affluent Britain 1957–1964* (Manchester: Manchester University Press, 2005); Hennessy, P., *Having It so Good* (London: Penguin, 2006); Thomas, N., 'Will the real 1950s please stand up?', *Cultural and Social History*, 5: 2 (2008), pp. 227–35; and Mort, F., *Capital Affairs* (New Haven: Yale University Press, 2010).

52 Edward Heath reported in *The Times*, 15 May 1973. Heath was speaking in reference to the allegations of corruption and fraud in relation to the businessman, Tiny Rowland, and the London and Rhodesian Mining and Land Company, subsequently known as Lonrho.

53 Johnston, M., 'Right and wrong in British politics: fits of morality in comparative perspective', *Polity*, 24: 1 (1991), pp. 1–25.

54 *The Times*, 26 April 1860.

55 Dame Evelyn Sharp quoted in Sharpe, L.J., 'Elected representatives in local government', *British Journal of Sociology*, 13: 3 (1962), pp. 189–209.

56 Brand, J., 'Party organisation and the recruitment of councillors', *British Journal of Political Science*, 3: 4 (1973), pp. 473–86.

3 Graft in Glasgow and Labour's ascendancy 1933–68

> In aristocratic governments, those who are placed at the head of affairs are rich men, who are desirous only of power. In democracies, statesmen are poor and have their fortunes to make. The consequence is that in aristocratic states the rulers are rarely accessible to corruption and have little craving for money, while the reverse is the case in democratic nations.
>
> Alexis de Tocqueville, *Democracy in America* (1835)[1]

Before the First World War, Glasgow was ruled if not by an aristocracy but at least by a wealthy and urban patriciate which was recruited from a narrow social and religious range. It dominated the Corporation, the Royal Infirmary, the Merchant's House, the Chamber of Commerce and the Clyde Trust. In 1909, it numbered probably 271 individuals of whom less than half held a single office and only eighteen who held two or three offices. It was also very wealthy and cohesive, and in addition to its political power, it also dominated the social and cultural life in the city. It had shaped the urban fabric with an austere 'decorum' to reflect its ambitions and aspirations.[2] The city fathers' temple of achievements celebrated industry, commerce and endeavour, and they were able to promote an image of civic probity and exert a singular 'moral authority' over the life of the city.[3] However, by the first decade of the twentieth century, the Glasgow middle classes from whom the elite recruited became increasingly detached from the life of the city. This process of detachment was followed by a reconfiguration of Glasgow's politics which was hastened by the First World War and its immediate aftermath. Franchise reform in 1918 made politics more democratic and allowed lower middle-class and working-class groups into the political arena. Nor should we overlook the Irish Treaty of 1921 which undermined the *raison d'être* of the Unionist Party in Scotland and in Glasgow in particular. The vacation of civic space by the old elite left a more democratic space which was filled by the working classes and their organisations. This new political class contained men who 'lived by politics' but who had not been schooled in the traditions of civic probity that had been the ideal of the outgoing elite. Further, the new politics was marked increasingly by sectarian strife and class polarisation. Additionally, a deteriorating economic environment intensified competition for scarce public resources, principally council houses, and this was fertile ground for the growth of corruption.[4]

At the moment when Labour first achieved control of Glasgow Corporation in 1933, seemingly the democratic dividend of the post-1918 settlement, the Secretary of State for Scotland, Sir Geoffrey Collins, appointed a Tribunal of Inquiry to investigate allegations of bribery and corruption in the affairs and administration of the Corporation. In the autumn of 1941, the leader of the Progressives (Conservatives) on Glasgow Corporation, John McSkimming, put forward a motion calling for an inquiry into allegations of corruption into the city's affairs. He was surprisingly supported by Patrick Dollan, the Socialist Lord Provost.[5] Dollan was attacked by his own party who accused him of prejudging the issue. McSkimming's motion was countered by a filibuster from the Socialist councillors, and there was no further debate.[6]

Although Labour had become the majority party on the Corporation in 1933, its success did not create a stable political environment. Glasgow's reputation in the 1930s was one of turbulence and violence fuelled in the popular press by lurid stories of gang fights and violence.[7] The city was compared to Chicago fuelling images of social breakdown and criminality. The political system, too, was distorted by 'graft'.[8] Interestingly, the cases in question – bribes and inducements for houses and market lettings – were referred to readily as 'graft', a term deployed freely in America to the practice of politicians milking their office for personal gain.[9] Was Glasgow an American-style city with American-style problems, principally corruption? Such a comparison does encourage reflection, and so we should look at Glasgow's substantial corruption cases and explain them in terms of the city's political culture as well as its economic and social structure. Additionally, we should recognise that Glasgow's political culture was shaped by a broader set of factors that emanated from Glasgow's society, which was riven by political and social conflicts centred around, initially, an ideological dispute between mainstream Labour and the Independent Labour Party (ILP). Secondly, the economic crisis of the west of Scotland and Glasgow especially determined that every human transaction – a sale of goods, a request for a liquor licence, an application for a council house, the renting of a market pitch and tendering for a corporation contract – was bounded by a series of social and cultural parameters. These included the powerful forces of sectarianism which commanded such loyalty. The structures of political patronage which flowed from these circumstances produced a command and control system which meant that political activists came to regard bribes and rewards as legitimate tools for the exercise of power and the sustenance of loyalty from various client groups. These were determined by class, religion and ethnicity. Further, the bribe system represented a bargain: the briber might get a new council house, and the councillor got some expenses that he might spread to other members of his faction so that they could indeed 'live by politics'. Thus, the bribes system helped to cement a series of allegiances to the political constituency without and to the members of the political class within. So, in 1933, it had come to light that a Glasgow bailie, James Strain, had secured bribes for the letting of stances at the Glasgow meat market. The bribery case attracted considerable attention so much so that parliament resolved, eventually, to set up an investigation under the terms of the Tribunals of Inquiry (Evidence) Act 1921. Thus, the power of the central state bore down on the autonomy of local government in a new and remarkable way. It was the first occasion when the power of the Tribunal system had been used to investigate a local government corporation. The *Glasgow Tribunal* heard evidence from forty-one witnesses and scrutinised a whole range of Corporation activities, not just the letting of stances in the meat market but also the arrangements for the licensing of public houses, the letting of corporation houses as well as the operations of the rating and valuation department. James Strain and Alexander Ritchie, a Glasgow councillor, had already been arrested and were charged in the Glasgow High Court with corruption under the Public Bodies (Corrupt Practices) Act 1889. Strain was found guilty, fined £50 and forbidden to hold public office for three years. His crime was judged particularly 'heinous' because he had suggested the bribe and also the sum of £50.[10] The case against Ritchie was dropped.[11]

Why did the Strain and Ritchie case, on the face of it an example of petty corruption that was not infrequent in many corners of local government, attract so much attention? First, Glasgow was an important regional centre and in some senses the capital of the west of Scotland. It was a major port and financial centre with its own stock exchange its wealth built on coal, iron, ships and steel. Between 1920 and 1935, however, Glasgow's economy endured acute crisis. The factors which had produced such wealth now became burdens as world trade contracted and new competitors came on to the world market. Glasgow's economy failed to diversify sufficiently, and by the 1930s, it was designated a region in need of government assistance under the terms of the Special Areas Act 1934. Thus, its high status profile within the British state and in the Scottish nation in particular made the apparent prevalence of corruption a matter of grave concern. A case of apparently 'white' corruption had turned 'black'. Additionally, the unrest that had beset Glasgow during and immediately after the First World War meant that it probably figured highly in the anxiety register of government ministers. It should be recalled that the arrangements for the government of Scotland within the British state were tightly prescribed. Scotland's legal system had retained its particular character since the Act of Union in 1707, but in 1885 the office of Secretary of State for Scotland was resuscitated, and a Scottish Office and Scottish Standing Committee based at Westminster were also established to consider specifically

Scottish Bills although it was not until 1937 that the Scottish Office was moved to Edinburgh.[12] This was a symbolic change, but perhaps it was also a consequence of the fact that Scottish affairs, including the Glasgow corruption scandal, in the 1930s were taking up so much parliamentary time. Perhaps that, too, was one of the more perverse successes of the ILP's sustained campaign on the scandal.

In political terms, Glasgow's apparently vigorous Liberal tradition had disintegrated under the pressures of the First World War. The War had been an acute crisis for Glasgow, and it experienced bitter industrial unrest as well as its famous rent strike. Its apparent revolutionary potential was hailed by Lenin calling it the 'Petrograd of the west'. Finally, the Battle of George Square on 31 January 1919 came to 'encapsulate the image of 'Red Clydeside'.[13] The Unionist MP for Springburn, Fred MacQuisten, demonised the leaders of the George Square protest, Emanuel Shinwell and William Gallagher, claiming that the unrest had been fomented by foreign influences.[14] Nevertheless, Labour representation had already begun to make its mark before the First World War and Glasgow's Labour movement sustained its momentum throughout the 1920s. This was fraught with ideological conflict within the Labour movement itself as has been aptly demonstrated by McKinlay and Morris.[15] It was the first British city to secure an outright Labour majority in municipal politics in 1933. However, although the Labour group was the largest group on the Corporation the internecine conflict between the ILP and Labour produced seemingly intractable difficulties. Indeed, Sir Robert Horne, the Unionist politician who represented Glasgow Hillhead, capitalised on these circumstances taunting Labour for its fractious disputes.[16] Thus, the post-1960s argument that corruption occurs in single-party fiefdoms is rather difficult to accept in Glasgow's case in the 1930s. Glasgow had enjoyed, since the late nineteenth century, a reputation for civic efficiency, and, despite a propensity for sectarianism, the city fathers of the Liberal tradition had established a stern ethic that promoted the common good by which they had been able, apparently, to triumph over the 'excesses of partisanship'.[17] By the Edwardian period, Glasgow had been feted as a model of 'civic excellence' and on a par with Birmingham for its planning, programmes of improvement and civic pride. Laski's eulogistic thinking on the virtues of local government was probably inspired in part by the example of Glasgow, and Laski's views had already been anticipated by the American political scientist, Albert Shaw, who had claimed that Glasgow was a 'guiding light' for others to follow.[18] Thus, Glasgow's powerful social elite had by the beginning of the twentieth century been able to promote an image of civic probity. 'The venerable corporation of the Clyde' had achieved much: the Glasgow Exhibition in 1888, second city of Empire, tramways, the People's Palace on Glasgow Green and much more[19]. However, those certainties had begun to break up at the beginning of the twentieth century. First because the growth of Liberal Unionism fractured the solidity of the social and political elite and second because the process of suburbanisation began to detach the upper middle class from the affairs of the city. This was demonstrated electorally with Liberal Unionist success in suburban greater Glasgow. In parliamentary terms, traditional Liberalism had collapsed by 1931 when it was unable to field a single candidate in any of the fifteen Glasgow divisions. Glasgow society also became uniquely polarised by the issue of the Irish Catholic vote which had been greatly enlarged following the establishment of universal male suffrage in 1918. Its upshot was that whereas Glasgow's elite had been dynamic in the mid-nineteenth century, it became increasingly, after 1886, less and less adaptable before withering away after 1922. The political vacuum created by its demise was filled in part by organised Labour, but it was by no means a coherent and unified force, and ultimately it failed to deliver.[20] One consequence of that failure was the revival of a Scottish Home Rule movement in the 1930s. Hostility between Labour and the more radical ILP could in fact produce conditions of a 'blocked political system' making an environment conducive to bribery.[21] Working-class politics was still marked by the traditions of Orange Protestantism, and the ideological disputes that it engendered helped no doubt to create the conditions for right-wing groups such as the Scottish Protestant League (SPL) to gain impetus in Glasgow. Thus, in the municipal elections of 1932, the League gained three seats capturing working-class and lower middle-class votes in Shettleston and Calton. It also succeeded in the more middle-class Kinning ward at the expense of the Moderates. Nevertheless, the Moderates hung on to their working majority.[22]

Against this legacy of civic probity and good government, the manifestations of corruption in Glasgow were shocking to politicians and social leaders alike. The apparent slide of a city once praised as a model of civic administration to one that was mired in graft and corruption was possibly, however, misleading. There had in fact been cases of corruption in the nineteenth century including the infamous City of Glasgow Bank crash whose directors, including two Glasgow Corporation councillors – John Stewart and William Taylor – were found guilty of false accounting with the intent to defraud. The story reflected badly on Glasgow Corporation with *The Scotsman* thundering that the crash had caused 'widespread ruin'.[23] For the most part, however, Glasgow's politics were clean although the political rhetoric that periodically marked the clashes between the temperance movement and the drink interest might have suggested otherwise. In 1909, Sir Samuel Chisholm, a former Lord Provost of Glasgow, delivered the annual lecture at the United Free Church Assembly: 'The Relation of the Drink Habit and the Drink Traffic to our Civic and National Life'. It was all bad news asserted Chisholm who gave his audience instances of his life on the magistrate's licensing bench including being offered bribes of up to £600 as well as being invited to go on holiday in April when the bench sat to consider new applications and licence renewals. 'The shadow of the licensing bench hung over practically every municipal election', he claimed, and he advocated that licensing should be removed from the local control of municipalities and magistrates.[24] Indeed, municipal election campaigns were marked by hostile exchanges between rival candidates of the temperance and drink factions, often resulting in election petitions and suits for slander. A favoured tactic of the drink interest was to assert that professed teetotallers had been seen drunk.[25] By the 1930s, the nature of the conduct of the debate changed so that McGovern's campaign became a *cause célèbre* that polarised opinion in a new and dramatic way.

Why was the ILP to the forefront of the campaign for an inquiry? In part it was down to McGovern who had been expelled from his local constituency party for irregularities in his selection process in the by-election of that year. It was said that he had used 'trade union delegates with forged credentials to vote him in at the selection meeting'.[26] Nevertheless, he contested successfully a subsequent general election as an ILP candidate and held on to Shettleston in 1935 and 1945 despite opposition from the official Labour Party. Thus, making the clarion call for an inquiry was a way of clearing his name and presenting himself as a clean candidate and a champion of probity. Secondly, McGovern's stance was of course integral to the campaign led by Jimmy Maxton to disaffiliate the ILP from Labour, successful in 1932. The disaffiliation campaign was central to the ILP strategy to present itself as the face of 'ethical socialism'[27] following Ramsay MacDonald's decision to form a National Coalition government with Conservatives and Liberals in 1931. It was seen in Scottish Labour circles as an act of betrayal. Significantly, the two accused in the Glasgow corruption scandal of 1933, Strain and Ritchie, were not members of the ILP. The stridency of McGovern's campaign and his determination to be seen as an advocate of civic probity complemented the ILP's wider claim to ethical socialism and ideological purity. Thus, the corruption of a Labour bailie and councillor as well as the subsequent inquiry became sticks with which the ILP could beat Labour. At the same time, it was a means whereby the ILP could assert a separate identity from a Labour Party that in Glasgow was a tainted failure. The protracted nature of the campaign was significant because it demonstrated clearly that ILP identity was neither established nor secure and it was being negotiated within Glasgow's politics by means of a campaign to expose corruption.[28] McGovern's role in bringing the case to the forefront may also have been a simple matter of opportunism and the fact that he was a 'headline grabber'.[29] Nonetheless, it exhibited an unquestionable political determination and resilience.

In Glasgow, the problems of corruption had first begun to surface in the 1920s when there were suggestions of bribery in the Springburn ward over the granting of drink licences. This had been reported in the press, but by 1929 further rumours had begun to circulate and the editors of the *Glasgow Evening News* and the *Glasgow Herald* became bolder in their headlines: 'Sinister Rumours that must be laid' and 'Glasgow's Reputation at Stake'.[30] These newspapers were the mouthpieces of Glasgow's business classes and the Procurator Fiscal initiated an investigation into the allegations that members of the Licensing Bench had been bribed.[31] Initially, William Leonard and John McGovern raised the matter at Glasgow's council meeting in January 1930. Leonard's request to suspend standing orders so that the matter might be discussed was ruled out of order by the chairman, bailie Jubb. The consequent 'disorderly scene' resulted in McGovern's expulsion from the council chamber.[32] The matter was then raised in the Commons in 1930 when John McGovern had made it the subject of his maiden speech, but at that time, there was insufficient evidence to take any further action. McGovern's inexperience with parliamentary protocol meant that he was easily rebutted by the Lord Advocate saying that the allegations of corruption 'were of the vaguest and most nebulous kind'. There was not, he claimed, a 'scintilla of evidence', and he rebuked both McGovern and Maxton for their 'vocal agitation' and their inability to bring forward evidence.[33] Nevertheless, the more right-wing MP for Renfrew West, Robert Forgan, also pressed the Secretary of State for Scotland to hold an inquiry. It was James Stewart, MP for St. Rollox, who successfully secured an answer from the Secretary of State, William Adamson, who eventually conceded the desirability of an inquiry.[34] However, the matter was not pursued. McGovern was undoubtedly compromised because he was in fact at odds with his own local party and the Glasgow Burgh Labour Party had called upon him to resign because of his persistent support for the Glasgow Green free speech campaign that was to lead to his arrest in October 1931. Thus, when the case of bailie Strain and the meat market bribes came to light in November 1932, there was much alarm. The Glasgow Labour Party resolved, somewhat reluctantly and under pressure from the ILP, that it should seek an inquiry and the Glasgow Corporation, too, agreed at last, if only to clear its name. The sense of outrage from social and political leaders was characterised by a stern anxiety: 'The affairs and administration of the city are doomed to disaster unless corruption is banished from it' claimed Lord Morrison, 'and it is the duty of every citizen to report at once any attempt at bribery and corruption'.[35] The Roman Catholic Archbishop of Westminster, Cardinal Bourne, went further in his *Lenten Pastorals* in 1934 saying, 'We used to pride ourselves upon the purity and incorruptibility of our public life and those entrusted with its guardianship. What we have learnt recently gives reason to fear that such pride is no longer justified'.[36] These views were shared across the political and social spectrum. McGovern weighed in, 'The civic administration of Glasgow was once the pride of the world, and we hope this inquiry will bring to light any disgraceful actions that might have been taken in the city'.[37] McGovern became the scourge of the Glasgow authorities when he raised the matter of three magistrates who had been caught drinking out of hours in a police raid on a number of public houses in the city as well as a magistrate who had sought £50 to 'assist' in a licence application.[38] He was also supported by

Jimmy Maxton and William Leonard, the latter claiming that there had been 'trafficking between the police and certain bookmakers'.[39]

The markets' case brought the matter to a head, and a vast range of Corporation activities were now under the microscope even though there were allegations of intimidation and blackmail of potential witnesses.[40] The Tribunal found that licensing administration was subject to sharp conflicts between brewers, distillers and publicans on the one hand and activists in the temperance movement on the other. It was not just the drink interest so tightly defined that had a stake in the granting of licences although they were excluded from the licensing bench, but it was also other small traders who supplied glasses, bottles, corks, fuel and those that provided painting, decorating and property repair. Surprisingly, though, the Inquiry cited only one instance of an attempt to bribe a magistrate but at the same time expressed its disappointment that more witnesses were not forthcoming on this matter. On the question of corporation houses which were in short supply, the Tribunal expressed one of its most damning comments stating that the administration of the letting of corporation houses displayed the 'prevalence of a regular system of venality'.[41] The Inquiry concluded that the 'selection of tenants to occupy [the] houses confers upon them advantages over ordinary citizens'.[42] There were some fifteen to eighteen officials in the housing department who controlled letting, and there was evidently 'ample scope for bribery'.[43] The legacy of Liberal reformism was apparent with preference being given to 'respectable' applicants, and no doubt sectarian bias was also in play. Subsequently, one housing officer was charged with receiving bribes when letting houses. Similarly, there were at least five instances in the rating and valuation department where rating assessors accepted bribes to lower rating valuations.[44] This was not a problem exclusive to Glasgow. Rating officers were often subject to intense pressure from householders to undervalue the rateable value of property.[45]

Glasgow markets – meat, fish and fruit – came in for special scrutiny. The complex arrangements for the letting of stances determined by their square footage and location as well as tariffs for meat carcasses and weights of other produce produced circumstances of Byzantine complexity, and it was clear that James Strain had a clear eye for an opportunity when there was fierce competition amongst traders. Indeed, it was acknowledged that his understanding of the detail was second to none, and therefore he was able to wield disproportionate influence. Strain had represented Gorbals ward since 1925 and had been promoted to bailie in 1930, and he had had been the long-standing convener of the markets committee. He was an experienced politician, and we know that he was member of the Corporation who exploited its expenses system to the full. Ritchie was less experienced and had represented the Ruchill ward. He also taught at the National Council of Labour Colleges, and in the 1931 General Election, he had successfully fought the Cathcart division. So they both had apparently acceptable credentials.[46]

The consequences of the Glasgow corruption scandals are difficult to chart. The moral disapprobation of Cardinal Bourne and the castigation of the Tribunal's chairman was a severe admonishment:

> There will be no real effective sanction unless it is recognised by each councillor and employee that he occupies in relation to the community a fiduciary position, violation of which by the solicitation of bribes constitute a serious breach of trust.[47]

However, Glasgow Corporation escaped lightly and was confident enough to resolve in September 1933 that there was nothing further to be done. The law took its course with Strain, Ritchie and the housing officers, Andrew Fairfull and William Forbes. The Corporation's reputation was nevertheless tainted, and attempts by its politicians to represent the city's interests at Westminster were weakened. The spirit of municipal socialism was retreating in the face of a more determined and centralised state, and Glasgow's attempts to secure a municipal savings bank and to establish its own tram and motor body manufacturing company were easily rebuffed by the government. First Secretary to the Treasury, Duff-Cooper, was dismissive of the proposal damning the Corporation's plans with faint praise:

> We all recognised and admire that civic spirit, but there is nothing more unfortunate than when the civic spirit of a great city is misled because that may lead to disaster. Anybody who studies history, not the ancient history but the recent history, of other countries, say of France and America, know the awful misfortunes which have befallen great cities owing to bad administration which creeps more easily into municipal government, than into the government of a great State. It is therefore dangerous to rely too much upon the civic spirit of a community to support ... their elected governors – temporarily elected governors – and to give powers which may not, in the long run, be used for people's good.[48]

The findings of the Tribunal provide a neat summary of corrupt activity in the city in the 1930s, but the Tribunal was unable to penetrate the dark corners of Glasgow's nether world of corruption. Glasgow was a tough city[49] and survival might often require some sharp practice. This was discernible in a broad range of areas.

The first area to consider is the matter of gambling which was regarded along with drink as one of the greatest social evils by the respectable classes. At the Annual Assembly of the Baptist Union of Scotland in 1925, the Reverend James Scott lamented that 'the practice of gambling was with us today in greater force than ever and it has grown to such gigantic proportions that it threatens to destroy our public morals'.[50] Drink and gambling vied with one another in the hierarchy of social evils as far as religious pressure groups were concerned. Thus, the Christian Union in 1931 in its Annual Report was pleased that the problems of drink had abated but was greatly alarmed about gambling citing the Irish sweepstake and the abuses of the totaliser. It called upon the churches and the Corporation to promote socially valuable activities as a distraction from gambling. The case of Agnes Miller who attempted to bribe a policeman who had intercepted a 'runner' in a case of street gambling indicates the degree of moral alarm that prevailed in respectable circles. 'Aggie the bookmaker' had attempted to bribe a policeman with the sum of ten shillings. She had form and was fined £25 and imprisoned for three months.[51] Agnes Miller's case alarmed the British Women's Temperance Association who were alert to the spread of gambling especially amongst women in a time of economic depression arguing that gambling was the 'saddest part of it all' as it led to the 'corruption of the women of the nation'.[52] Illegal betting also penetrated organised sport and especially football where players, particularly goalkeepers, were approached by agents of bookmakers and others with invitations to play badly and 'throw' a match. In 1926, a bookmaker's agent attempted to bribe Joe Shortt, Stenhousemuir's goalkeeper, to 'let his team down' with an inducement of £50.[53] The perpetrator was charged under the Prevention of Corruption Act (1906).

The policing of street gambling also exposed the police to the dangers of bribery, and there are numerous instances where the police were compromised. They also found ingenious ways of supplementing their incomes including the provision of information about street accidents which were passed to insurance agents enabling some constables to secure as much as thirty shillings a week. Insurance companies and solicitors employed agents to pursue information, and the cases of James Stewart and David Straiton revealed how lucrative insurance claims could be. The trials of Stewart and Straiton were reported avidly in the press, and full coverage was given to the evidence of Straiton's secretary, Elizabeth McCabe, who told the court how the information was obtained from the police and how the rewards were distributed. Stewart had made £770 and was charged under the 1906 Act and sent to prison for eighteen months. His professional career was destroyed. Straiton was imprisoned for six months.[54]

The struggle between the temperance movement and the drink interest was perhaps the longest running problem that benighted the civic life of Glasgow. The passion on the part of the temperance movement to limit and reduce drinking was met in turn by a resolute determination on the part of the drinks trade to preserve its livelihood. The drink trade was well organised, and the Scottish Licenses Mutual Insurance Association provided insurance compensation for publicans who had lost their licences. Between 1898 and 1934, it had dispersed £680,000 in compensation. The chairman of the Association, James Duff, complained that the present system of licensing was 'cruelly unjust'. He accused the licensing bench of having the 'power to cause loss without responsibility [and] where there is oppression that inevitably leads to bribery and corruption'.[55] The shopkeepers of Whiteinch, a 'dry' area in Glasgow, agreed as they complained to the Corporation and the Scottish Licensing Commission that they had lost trade as people went elsewhere.[56] The Tribunal had acknowledged this but, remarkably, found little evidence of bribery despite the number of court cases reported in the press. In McGovern's campaign for an inquiry, he cited the influence of the drink trade and the numerous attempts to bribe members of the licensing bench. The drink problem in Scotland and Glasgow in particular was such that Scottish MPs attempted to promote a bill enabling a local veto on drink licences. Its protagonist was Edwin Scrymgeour, an ardent prohibitionist and independent socialist, but his private members' bill was defeated by 137 to 18 in February 1931.[57] However, despite the fact that many of the activists in the Labour movement also subscribed to temperance values, the Labour movement was seen to be tainted by the influence of the drink. Thus, the West Scotland Temperance League, in 1933, launched a campaign 'to counteract the political activities of the liquor trade inside the Scottish Socialist movement'. According to one of its speakers, 'Drink was damaging the party. Labour members can be seen night after night in the House of Commons smoke room and soaking all the evening until they were stupid'.[58]

Glasgow's Labour politicians lived in this world of sharp practice, and they had acquired the levers of power at a critical moment in the city's history. The problems of industrial depression, poor health and an acute shortage of housing were perhaps the most notable challenges. Immediately prior to the markets case, the Corporation had published the expenses claims of bailies, councillors and employed officials. It showed that expenses for 1931–32 had fallen by £1770 to £11,011, a fall of some sixteen per cent. The largest claimant was Alexander Munroe, Chairman of the Gas Committee, who had claimed £134 but not far behind was bailie James Strain with £112.[59] Assuming that Strain's claim represented a reduction from the previous year, it may have prompted him to become more audacious in seeking bribes for stances at the meat market.

Outside of the hotly disputed matter of drink control, the other area most subject to pressure and ultimately sharp practice was in housing. This was the most acute social problem, and it was the area where Labour had failed to deliver. The Corporation had sought a boundary extension in 1930 to include the districts of Rutherglen and Bankhead with plans to build housing estates, but the extension was opposed by Lanarkshire County Council. However, it was clear from the Tribunal's report and the cases that emerged in the courts that corporation housing was an area fraught with danger. At the time of the Tribunal's hearing, there was a case in the High Court where a Corporation housing official, William Fairfull, was accused of soliciting bribes from would-be tenants of corporation houses.[60] Additionally, in June 1933, the case of William Forbes, an official in the City Improvements Department, came to light. Fairfull was charged on fifteen counts and found guilty in four cases. Fairfull had snared a number of agents or go-betweens, typically publicans, and a woman who would meet women applicants in tea rooms to collect their bribes.[61] It was the case of Forbes, however, that revealed the network of individuals who were involved in the bribery scheme. One would-be tenant sought a new council house on the Haghill scheme and applied in 1931 to be told by Forbes, 'The most of them are giving something. Can you give anything?' She paid ten shillings after visiting the scheme in August 1931 only to be pressed for a further payment of five shillings which she paid saying, ' I hope it chokes you'. The activities of Forbes involved bailies and councillors who were expected to 'recommend' potential tenants. Forbes' scheme also involved the participation of other corporation employees such as building site foreman, and he had recruited James Blyth, a site foreman, at the Drumoyne scheme, who told George Kellock who was in search of a house: 'One has to put his hands in his pockets if he wants a house'. Blyth sought a payment of £5. However, his brazen audacity encountered the redoubtable Alice Fraser who challenged him saying 'Do you not consider that a rotten system of doing things?' Blyth agreed and obviously went back to his master Forbes who then wrote to Alice Fraser's husband about the tenancy inserting 'P.S. Remember Friday first for settling account'.[62] There were of course other gifts required such as bottles of whiskey. Both Forbes and Fairfull were imprisoned, but revealingly their defence lawyer argued that because of the acute shortage of houses in the city, people would go to desperate lengths to get a house and that their evidence in the case had been 'engendered by disgruntled, disappointed and vindictive house hunters and evil minded scandal mongers'.[63]

The consequences of the corruption scandals did not adversely affect Labour's electoral position on the Corporation. In the elections of November 1933, the broad Labour grouping secured fifty-seven seats (Socialists forty-six and ILP eleven) against the Moderates' forty-nine seats. Thus, organised Labour had increased its representation from the position it had held in 1932. It may be that the scandal inspired an anti-Catholic backlash as the SPL won seven seats, but by 1936, the SPL was routed as the Moderates relaunched themselves as Progressives. Corruption, slander and accusations of administrative incompetence continued to mark the debate in Glasgow's politics at what might be considered a moment of Labour triumph – the election of Patrick Dollan as Lord Provost and the first politician of Irish descent to gain the position. Dollan was no stranger to prejudice, and earlier in his career in 1930, he had been forced to sue Andrew Rennie of Rennie Motors who had claimed that Dollan had accepted bribes from the Leyland Motors Company to supply buses to the Corporation. Dollan pursued a claim for slander and won.[64] In Dumbarton Burghs, the parliamentary agent of the respected David Kirkwood was imprisoned for three months for falsifying election expenses in 1936. In Glasgow's municipal elections of November 1937, Peter McIntyre had been successfully elected in the Anderston ward defeating John Ratcliffe of the Workers' Republican Party. During the contest, Ratcliffe made numerous claims including that McIntyre was in the pay of the Progressives and that his election expenses had been subsidised illegally by a local music hall manager. McIntyre decided to sue, claiming that Ratcliffe's speeches had slurred him [McIntyre] and represented him as someone of 'the lowest moral character and occupying himself with bribery and corruption'. The court found in McIntyre's favour and the Sheriff, in his summing up, stated that 'good reputation is a priceless possession' and awarded damages to McIntyre adding that 'evidence drawn from all local parties engaged in municipal politics vouches for your personal integrity and sincerity'. McIntyre's victory was important for the fact that he had followed Dollan's example and also because he won thus reasserting the principle of a 'fit and proper person' to conduct the affairs of the Corporation.[65]

It was however a short-lived interlude. In April 1941, bailie Hugh Campbell was charged with having received £120 to influence members of the licensing bench. At first sight, this might seem business as usual and the wrongdoings of the usual suspects – Labour bailies and councillors. Then in June 1941, two bailies and two councillors were arrested and charged under the Corruption Act of 1889. Three were Labour members and one an ILP bailie, Joseph Taylor. The usual suspect was Alexander Ritchie, councillor for Ruchill ward and Strain's pupil in the meat market case of 1933. The Sheriff refused bail indicating the seriousness of the case. At the same time, bailie Gemmell was imprisoned for twelve months for using his position and accepting a bribe to secure a promotion for an employee in the Baths Department. Gemmell not only accepted the bribe but passed a share of it to another councillor, Edward Hunter. But it was the case of Joseph Taylor, Alexander Ritchie and Thomas Wilson that attracted most attention. They were members of the Gas Committee and had travelled to London to consider a potential contract with a supplier of gas cookers that could be used in Corporation houses. Hugh Campbell who was already serving a sentence in the Barlinnie prison was also on the trip and now came and gave evidence against his fellows. Campbell at his trial said that he wanted to clear his conscience and to 'clear the corruption that is going on in Glasgow'. Campbell's evidence cited Ritchie as the ringleader: 'Here we are walking around with an order for a quarter of a million in our pockets and there seems to be nothing doing.' Subsequently at a dinner organised by the chairman of the gas cooker company, Campbell told the chairman that things would have to be 'squared' if he was to get the contract. Campbell asked for a payment of £2,000 and this was to be shared amongst the four members of the Gas Committee. Under cross-examination, Campbell said, 'It is the usual thing. It is accepted as a matter of fact'.[66] They all received prison sentences with Ritchie and Taylor each receiving eighteen months. The Sheriff said that Wilson was guilty of a 'grave offence against public morality' and only his age and ill-health saved him from a longer sentence.[67] Patrick Dollan welcomed the sentences saying that cleaning up dishonesty was necessary, but he was worried because 'there are still rumours circulating in the whispering galleries, but unless those who make statements come forward with evidence, the police and the courts can do nothing'.

It was in this atmosphere that John McSkimming, leader of the Progressives, came forward at the council meeting in October 1941 with a quite remarkable speech in which he claimed that there was no councillor of experience who was unaware of how easy it was to be dishonest. He went on:

> I have more than a suspicion that there is a permanent organization existing in Glasgow with contacts in this Chamber, and the function of that organization is to ascertain quietly and subtly whether new councillors and new magistrates who come on the scene are touchable or are not touchable.[68]

Whether McSkimming was aware of the work of Elliot Ness and his eleven 'untouchables' in Chicago is not clear. It was certainly widely reported in the British press. It does seem clear, though, that he believed that the drink trade was a source of corruption in Glasgow's public life. He went on to call for a determined effort to break 'the organisation' as he put it, and he called for cross-party support as all members of the council were 'chafing under the slur of recent trials'.[69] The Labour group through Hector McNeill recalled the futility of the Inquiry of 1933 and asked that the Town Clerk consult with the Secretary of State and invite people to come forward with evidence. It caused a fierce rebuttal from McSkimming claiming that the Socialists were only interested in 'window dressing' and that they were trying to 'bury the corpse with a few flowers'. The Labour side triumphed defeating McSkimming's motion by fifty-three votes to thirty-seven. Labour's reputation was clearly tarnished, and the Glasgow Chamber of Commerce called for decisive action recommending new arrangements for the controlling of corporation contracts via a separate committee which would superintend the specialist committees.

Meanwhile, Joseph Taylor mounted an appeal against his sentence, but Lord Wark dismissed it saying that it was necessary to secure the 'preservation of the purity of municipal government'. He hoped, too, that the Corporation would take steps to prevent future cases of corruption.[70] The Corporation went through the motions and the Town Clerk approached the Secretary of State, Tom Johnston, who responded by saying that the statements of evidence that he had received did not warrant criminal proceedings.[71] However, he did recommend that Licensing Bench sessions should be conducted in public as a means of 'restoring public confidence in the civic administration of Glasgow'. *The Scotsman* thought that it would have little effect suggesting instead that members of the Bench should be forbidden to visit premises that were applying for a licence. The newspaper's editorial though asserted that the Corporation 'has not given the appearance of being possessed by any whole hearted desire to probe the matter'.[72] The Corporation's reputation was now in tatters and the Chairman of the Scottish Temperance Alliance, Daniel Lamont, claimed that the Corporation was steeped in 'graft'. He was also critical of Johnston calling his response 'feeble'. Lamont was committed to the principle that drink licences should not be controlled by local authorities, and the Alliance set up a special committee to wage a campaign on this issue.[73] Labour's George Smith huffed and puffed about 'tittle-tattle' and 'hearsay stories in smoke-filled rooms' but did advocate that party organisation needed to become more disciplined and employ more robust procedures when selecting candidates. Labour was now on the defensive.

The consequences of Glasgow's corruptions stretching back to at least the late 1920s were not immediately discernible, but certainly Labour's status was impaired. The Progressives were now much more confident and able to go on the offensive. The Special Committee that had been set up to review the question of contracting in particular was roundly attacked by the Reverend R.W. Waddelow, a Progressive councillor, who accused it of incompetence and cynicism. There was certainly complacency on the Labour side with Adam McKinlay who had been a member of the Special Committee when he defended the Committee's recommendations, essentially no change, when he claimed that the 'Council was now a Garden of Eden compared with what it was several years ago'. He argued that it was up to the integrity of councillors 'backed up ably by the local presses'.[74] This did represent a change on Labour's part as at the height of the scandal in 1933 when the Tribunal met the Labour group and the ILP had blamed the press for whipping up the scandal. The *Glasgow Evening Times* and the *Glasgow Herald* were no friends of Labour, and the Beaverbrook press in Scotland, principally the *Scottish Sunday Express* and the *Daily Record*, showed 'scant sympathy' for Labour's troubles.[75] Tom Johnston had also become impatient and exhorted the Corporation to seek technical advice on the management of contracts, and he wrote to the Glasgow Town Clerk saying that the smooth running of local administration and the elimination of corruption required 'a high standard of social responsibility through the community'.[76] Corruption then had a corrosive effect on Labour's ability to deal with the social problems – poor housing, unemployment and high infant mortality rates – that beset Glasgow in the 1930s. The idealism and optimism that had arisen from Labour's triumphs in parliamentary elections in 1922 and the capturing of the Corporation in 1933 were becoming increasingly open to doubt and disappointment. In the municipal elections of November 1947, Labour lost its overall control of the Corporation. The Progressives were now resurgent and confident. Labour knew as one councillor put it that it would 'have to stand on its own legs' as the support of traditional allies such as ILP and other independents was no longer a certainty. Struggles over the chairmanship of key committees were now the order of the day, and when John Ratcliffe, the councillor for Anderston ward since 1921, resigned the Labour whip over a dispute to reconstitute the Education Committee, then Labour's grip was broken.[77]

Tom Johnston was made a freeman of the City of Dundee in 1948 where he had been a former MP. In his acceptance speech, he made a plea for the teaching of citizenship in schools. This was an echo of the thinking of Lord Simon of Wythenshawe, but it had a special resonance in Scotland: 'Good citizenship adequately inculcated in our schools would be the antidote to black marketing [and] the thieving of goods. Not until the good citizen was recognised as the primary end of education would we be able to turn out really efficient workmen, scientists, technicians and administrators'.[78] Was he thinking of Glasgow when he made this plea? He was no doubt aware that Hector McNeill, Glasgow's Lord Provost, was trapped in crisis talks with Glasgow's municipal employees in a dispute over pension and holiday payments, and 2,600 council employees were on strike.[79] Ultimately, Labour had failed to solve key questions of reform although its bailies and councillors were not averse to extracting from the system the perks of office. Thus, the traditional picture that corruption in Scotland had been associated with Tory notables[80] in the smaller burghs was now replaced by an image that corruption and specifically graft was a Labour area of expertise.

Glasgow after 1947 remained a city marked by corruption and graft. The persistence of sectarian friction over access to public housing was a key pressure point, but whether it was used to generate electoral advantage is difficult to tell. Chronic overcrowding in the inner city meant that Glasgow Corporation officials in the Housing Department still wielded immense discretionary power. It has been suggested, for example, that working-class Catholics were sent to the Blackhill scheme.[81] In some respects, this segregation was a function of inter-war approaches to sectarian control by city officials who used notions of respectability and acceptable social behaviour as yardsticks when making housing allocations. Such criteria inevitably loaded the dice in favour of Protestants. Thus, finding a way round the system, as in Belfast too, by bribery and influence was not a surprising outcome.[82] At the same time, the persistence of denominational schooling may have sustained patterns of sectarian spatial settlement. Overall, after the Second World War, Catholics made up approximately one-third of the city's population, but they were concentrated in the districts of Arden, Balornock, Garthamlock, Greenfield and Springing. Protestants dominated Auldhouse, Eastwood, Blairdardie, Merrylee and Simshill.[83] Thus, there was no declared policy to enforce residential segregation except for school preference, but bribery may have been the unknown factor. Further, once schools were established, their location affected advertisements for employment such as janitors and clerical staff, and as has already been demonstrated, this was an area ripe for patronage and corruption.

Given Glasgow's size and economic dominance of the Clyde region, it was not surprising that regional planning gained increasing momentum. The Clyde Valley Regional Plan was published in 1946.[84] Labour drew support from both working-class Catholics and Protestants alike. The population of the city's inner wards reduced dramatically between 1951 and 1971, and the eight wards with the largest Catholic presence fell from 69,000 to 13,000. Glasgow's population was decanted to the peripheral estates of Easterhouse, Drumchapel and Castlemilk and to the new towns such as East Kilbride which the Glasgow Corporation fiercely resisted. Other destinations included Glenrothes, Cumbernauld, Livingston and Irvine.[85] Further, the proportion living in public sector housing of the Glasgow population living in council housing was sixty-four per cent in 1979, whereas for the rest of Scotland, it was fifty-four per cent and only thirty-two per cent for the United Kingdom as a whole.

During a period of such massive change, it was not surprising that traditional patterns of loyalty persisted, particularly in employment. Dock labour and patterns of skilled labour in shipbuilding operated gang systems. Here patronage was endemic and sectarian. Thus, there was a culture of subjectivity, and patterns of loyalty became increasingly entrenched. This extended to housing lists and also patterns of employment in Glasgow Corporation. The Scottish Office endeavoured to regulate this activity but with limited success. Glasgow Corporation remained highly resistant so much so that the Scottish Office sought to reduce Glasgow's power and it used the Scottish Special Housing Association (SSHA) which built 100,000 houses between 1937 and 1987. Thus, the SSHA was used along with Treasury support to take away Glasgow Corporation's management of housing, and this may have been beneficial in terms of a check on corruption. Nevertheless, Glasgow did develop Pollok, Drumchapel, Castlemilk and Easterhouse, but there is evidence to suggest that there were sectarian quotas as well as higher rents for houses built by the SSHA and in the new towns. The rebuilding of the Clyde region then provided a ready-made means of much social filtering.[86] Glasgow Corporation still controlled twenty-nine comprehensive redevelopment areas, and shortage of land enabled further social and sectarian engineering.

In such circumstances, it was not surprising then that there were further episodes of corruption. In 1968, the Glasgow police began investigations into a 'graft syndicate' involving councillors and officials. There were allegations of bribes for contracts, planning consents and liquor licences. The Lord Provost, Douglas Glen, thought the claims were 'very disturbing'.[87] George Leslie, leader of the SNP on Glasgow Corporation, asked The Times to substantiate its claims. There was in fact no overall control of the council following the May 1968 elections, and Glen sought tripartite support from Labour, Progressives and SNP for an inquiry. The debate in the council chamber became heated, and Councillor Donald Liddle proclaimed that 'people should be pinned if they are true, or their names should be cleared if they are not true'. The Glasgow Town Clerk subsequently drafted a letter to The Times. The Inquiry lasted eighteen months and did not report until February 1970.[88]

The Inquiry rejected the existence of a graft syndicate, but James Dougherty, an official in the Planning Department, was charged under the Corrupt Practices Act of 1889. It was, according to NALGO, a 'damning slur on their integrity as public servants'. Nevertheless, two Labour councillors and John Scott, a whiskey dealer, were found guilty of being involved in a corrupt transaction to issue a drink licence. Additionally, councillor John Paterson, aged seventy-two, was also found guilty for numerous dealings with Glasgow companies. Councillor James Reilly (Labour) was also prosecuted and gaoled for eighteen months as he had accepted £100 as inducements to influence housing tenancies.[89] At the same time, the Inquiry reported that the Corporation had overspent by £2.5 million on a housing scheme planned for £5.95 million. The Lord Provost Douglas Glen expressed his dismay, 'The whole investigation has had a significant effect on civic life here. I only hope we can now forget what has happened and look forward to the future with more confidence'.[90]

The Glasgow pattern of corruption belies a traditional view that corruption occurs where there was an established oligarchy, at least in the early period of Labour's ascendancy 1933–47. Rather, it suggests that the overthrow of an older traditional oligarchy and the opening up of the political system generated upward social mobility for Labour councillors of working-class backgrounds who when they arrived in the corridors of power were easily seduced by its grand associations. Further, a blocked political system as demonstrated by the ILP–Labour split encouraged corruption as councillors sought to cement the loyalty of their client groups by means of favours, bribery and corruption. Nevertheless, the ideological fissure that opened up between the ILP and mainstream Labour provided the former with ample motive to expose wrongdoing. Finally, in the post-war era of reconstruction, conditions had changed: between 1945 and 1968, Labour dominated the council chamber for twenty years out of twenty-four. Labour had become a new oligarchy that remained attached to corruption as a device to exert and enjoy power. Glasgow's painful process of deindustrialisation was followed by central state intervention to shore up the city's infrastructure, and the provision of public goods, such as housing, meant that money flowed. Those who brokered the distribution of those resources would often regard some rake-off as just desserts for their own efforts.

Notes

1 Tocqueville, *Democracy in America* (1994), p. 225.
2 Trainor, R., 'The elite', in Fraser, W.H. and I. Maver (eds.), *Glasgow*, vol. II, 1839–1912, (Manchester: Manchester University Press, 1996), pp. 255–57.
3 Nenadic, S., 'The Victorian middle classes', in Fraser and Maver, *Glasgow*, p. 292.
4 Paterson, I., 'Sectarianism and municipal housing allocation in Glasgow', *Scottish Affairs*, 39 (2002), pp. 39–53.
5 In the interwar period, the traditional Unionists in Scottish politics who supported the Act of Union of 1707 had adopted the title Moderates in Glasgow municipal politics, and in 1936 they adopted the title Progressives. Similarly, the Scottish Labour Party generally adopted the title Socialists.
6 *The Scotsman*, 17 October 1941.
7 *Sunday Mail*, 3 February 1935. See also McArthur, A. and H. Long, *No Mean City* (London: Longman Green, 1935).
8 *The Scotsman*, 2 March 1933; 3 March 1933; 17 March 1933; 31 March, 7 April, 11 April 1933; *Glasgow Evening News*, 31 May 1933.
9 *The Shorter Oxford English Dictionary* (1983) 'Graft' is identified as US slang dating from 1889 and specifically in connection to illicit gains or profits in connection with political or municipal business.
10 *Glasgow Tribunal Inquiry* (1933), Cmd., 4361, para. 8a, p. 7.
11 *The Times*, 6 February 1933.
12 Devine, T.M., *The Scottish Nation 1700–2007* (London: Penguin, 2006), p. 660.
13 Maver, I., *Glasgow* (Edinburgh: Edinburgh University Press, 2000), p. 230.
14 Emanuel Shinwell was of Jewish descent, and William Gallagher was of Irish Catholic descent.
15 McKinlay, A. and R.J. Morris, *The ILP on Clydeside 1893–1932: From Foundation to Disintegration* (Manchester: Manchester University Press, 1991).
16 *The Times*, 6 November 1930.
17 Maver, I., 'Politics and power in the Scottish city: Glasgow Town Council in the nineteenth century', in Devine, T.M. (ed.), *Scottish Elites: Proceedings of the Scottish Historical Studies Seminar at the University of Strathclyde 1991–92* (Edinburgh: John Donald, 1994), pp. 98–130.

18 Maver, I., in Devine, *Scottish Elites*, pp. 98–130; Smyth, J., 'Resisting labour: union-ists, liberals and moderates in Glasgow between the wars', *The Historical Journal*, 46: 2 (2003), pp. 375–401.

19 *Glasgow Herald*, 27 May 1890.

20 Fraser, W.H., *Scottish Popular Politics: From Radicalism to Labour* (Edinburgh: Polygon, 2002), p. 159.

21 Ginsborg, *Italy and Its Discontents* (2001), pp. 137–78.

22 *The Scotsman*, 22 October 1932.

23 *The Scotsman*, 8 November 1878, 3 February 1879. See also Maver, in Devine, *Scottish Elites*, 98–130; and Checkland, S., *Scottish Banking: A History 1695–1973* (Edinburgh: John Donald, 1975), pp. 471–81.

24 *The Scotsman*, 16 November 1909.

25 *The Scotsman*, 24 March 1909, 18 December 1909 and 16 March 1912.

26 Knox, W., *Scottish Labour Leaders 1918–1939* (Edinburgh: Mainstream Publishing, 1984), p. 177; and Maver, I., 'McGovern, John 1887–1968', *Oxford Dictionary of National Biography*, www.odnb.com, visited on 18 January 2011.

27 Fraser, *Scottish Popular Politics*, p. 162.

28 See Brown, A., D. McCrone and L. Paterson (eds.), *Politics and Society in Scotland* (Basingstoke: Macmillan, 1996), pp. 197–209.

29 Knox, *Scottish Labour Leaders*, p. 176.

30 *Glasgow Herald*, 31 May 1929.

31 *The Scotsman*, 14 December 1929.

32 *The Scotsman*, 24 January 1930.

33 *Hansard*, HC Debates, 2 July 1930, vol. 240, cc. 1959–60.

34 *The Scotsman*, 12 February 1930.

35 Lord Morrison quoted in *The Times*, 22 February 1933.

36 *The Times*, 12 February 1934.

37 *Hansard*, HC Debates, 10 April 1933, vol. 276, cc. 2336–42.

38 *Hansard*, HC Debates, 1 June 1933, vol. 278, cc. 2060–1.

39 *Hansard*, HC Debates, 6 April 1933, vol. 276, cc. 1907–8.

40 *Hansard*, John McGovern, HC Debates, 10 April 1933, vol. 276, cc. 2336–42.

41 *Glasgow Tribunal*, para. 5, 4.

42 *Ibid.*, para. 7c, p. 6.

43 *Ibid.*

44 *Ibid.*, para. 8c, p. 9.

45 *The Times*, 11 December 1930.

46 *The Scotsman*, 26 November 1932, 28 November 1932, 29 November 1932, 3 December 1932.

47 *Glasgow Tribunal*, para. 11, p. 12.

48 *The Scotsman*, 27 March 1935; *Hansard*, HC Debates, vol. 299, cc. 1820–77.

49 MacArthur, A. and H. Long, *No Mean City* (London: Wells and Gardner, 1940); Thompson, G., *Caledonia or the Future of the Scots* (London: Kegan Paul, Trench and Tubner, 1927); and Robertson, G., *Gorbals Doctor* (London: Jarrolds, 1970).

50 *The Scotsman*, 21 October 1925.

51 *The Scotsman*, 26 January 1937, 28 January 1937.

52 *The Scotsman*, 27 March 1931.

53 *The Scotsman*, 26 December 1925; 9 February 1926. Former players of Hamilton Academicals had attempted to bribe the captain of the club to play badly in a match against Leith Athletic in 1931; *The Scotsman*, 6 January 1931.

54 *The Scotsman*, 29 June 1938.
55 *The Scotsman*, 30 September 1937.
56 *The Scotsman*, 18 February 1930.
57 *The Scotsman*, 5 February 1931; and Knox, *Scottish Labour Leaders*, pp. 239–43.
58 *The Scotsman*, 15 May 1933.
59 *The Scotsman*, 26 October 1932.
60 *The Scotsman*, 7 April 1933.
61 *The Scotsman*, 6 September 1933.
62 *The Scotsman*, 12 September 1933, 13 September 1933, 14 September 1933.
63 *The Scotsman*, 14 September 1933.
64 *The Scotsman*, 10 November 1930.
65 *The Scotsman*, 8 July 1938.
66 *The Scotsman*, 25 September 1941.
67 *The Scotsman*, 26 September 1941.
68 *The Scotsman*, 28 October 1941.
69 *The Scotsman*, 28 October 1941.
70 *The Scotsman*, 17 December 1941.
71 *The Scotsman*, 30 December 1941.
72 *The Scotsman*, 11 February 1942.
73 *The Scotsman*, 16 February 1942.
74 *The Scotsman*, 26 June 1942.
75 Maver, Glasgow, p. 253.
76 Tom Johnston, letter to Glasgow Town Clerk, quoted in *The Scotsman*, 20 July 1942.
77 *The Scotsman*, 8 November 1947.
78 *The Scotsman*, 17 November 1947.
79 *The Scotsman*, 29 November 1947.
80 Hutchinson, I., *A Political History of Scotland 1832–1924: Parties, Elections and Issues* (J. Donald, Edinburgh and Atlantic Highlands, New Jersey, 1986), p. 52.
81 Gallagher, T., *Glasgow – The Uneasy Peace: Religious Tension in Modern Scotland* (Manchester: Manchester University Press, 1987).
82 Paterson, 'Sectarianism in housing', pp. 39–53.
83 *Ibid*.
84 Abercrombie, P., *Clyde Valley Regional Plan, 1946: A Report Prepared for the Clyde Valley Regional Planning Committee* (1949).
85 Rodger, R., *Scottish Housing in the Twentieth Century* (Leicester: Leicester University Press, 1989).
86 *Ibid*.
87 *The Times*, 15 November 1968.
88 *The Times*, 27 February 1970.
89 *The Times*, 27 March 1969.
90 *The Times*, 27 February 1970.

4 Rebuilding the North Country: Poulson and Smith

> A luncheon or a drink or two, a little *savoir faire*
> I fix the Planning Officer, Town Clerk and the Mayor
> And if some preservationist attempts to interfere
> A dangerous structure notice from the Borough Engineer
> Will settle any buildings standing in our way –
> The modern style, sir, with respect, has really come to stay.
> John Betjeman, 'The executive' (1958)[1]

In 1972, John Poulson, a successful north of England architect, filed for bankruptcy. Consequently, he was charged with numerous counts of corruption and committed for trial at Leeds Crown Court. The case lasted for several months, and Poulson and twenty-one others were convicted. Poulson was sentenced to seven years imprisonment but was paroled in May 1977 having served three years. In his autobiography, *The Price*, published in 1981, he complained: 'I was their scapegoat'.[2] The consequences of the Poulson case were considerable: there were trials of numerous public servants and local politicians, including the Newcastle city boss, T. Dan Smith; a number of MPs, John Cordle and Albert Roberts, were disgraced; and the Home Secretary, Reginald Maudling, resigned in July 1972 when the Metropolitan Police began its investigation of Poulson.[3] Maudling had been a director of two of Poulson's companies and was intimately connected with plans to build a hospital on the island of Gozo for the Maltese government. Eventually, in July 1974, Harold Wilson conceded the establishment of a Royal Commission under the chairmanship of Lord Salmon to investigate the affair. Finally, the prosecution of T. Dan Smith exposed a network of corruption that spread across the north-east of England and included Andrew Cunningham, the chairman of Durham County Council and known variously as 'Mr Felling', as he was Chairman of Felling District Council; the 'godfather' of the north-east; and also Ted Short, Lord President of the Council and deputy leader of the Labour Party.[4] The Poulson case illustrates a significant feature of corrupt activity: its public revelation is often dependent on chance, but significantly it illustrates a key feature – corruption is often likely to occur where public and private markets meet.

It was standard in corruption trials for those found guilty to be chastised and shamed on the grounds that they had broken trust and practised treachery and that they had defamed the reputations of others as well as damaged the credibility of government institutions both national and local: 'To offer corrupt gifts strikes at the very foundation of our system. To accept them is a betrayal of trust', said Justice Waller when passing sentence on Poulson and George Pottinger, the civil servant in the Scottish Office who had assisted Poulson with the Aviemore tourist centre project in 1963.[5] Poulson's defence may have had some substance. 'I have been a fool surrounded by a pack of leeches'.[6] The defence of foolish generosity was sustained by his wife, Cynthia Poulson, in her interview in *Woman's Own* magazine shortly before her husband's parole in May 1977: 'John is probably the most generous man I know. Even now he spends the meagre wages he earns scrubbing out the prison library on lavish birthday and anniversary cards for me … Even I can see he was excessively stupid. But I can't regard him as a criminal. I see him not as a bad man but much more the victim of circumstances … I truly believe my husband was a scapegoat'.[7] Poulson himself sustained the 'scapegoat' claim in his autobiography, *The Price*, when he asserted that he was 'the victim of a legal and political machination with immense powers of censorship'.[8] These claims are often dismissed as the vitriolic outbursts of a defeated man, but in May 1974, Granada TV had broadcast 'Business in Gozo'. It was critical of the conduct of the Maltese government and alleged that Reginald Maudling had 'at times played a crucial role in securing the contracts for Poulson'.[9] Maudling took exception to the programme's claims and in September 1974 issued a writ for libel against Granada TV. The company appealed but Maudling was able to block a request from Granada that transcripts held by Poulson's bankruptcy trustee should be made available. Maudling's argument that he had given the evidence in confidence and that Granada TV were 'strangers to the case'[10] held sway. Maudling was able to resist requests that he should make available his books, files, papers and correspondence on the Gozo matter. Poulson's claim that he was the 'scapegoat' may then have some credence. From the outset, Maudling's political colleagues rallied around him. Thus, when the Cabinet discussed Poulson's claims in July 1972, and Maudling himself was required to leave the Cabinet room, the Attorney General, Sir Peter Rawlinson, asserted that Poulson's intent was 'to defame the Home Secretary and to involve him … in his [Poulson's] disgrace'. Sir Peter claimed that there was no evidence of 'any impropriety in his dealings with Mr Poulson'.[11] The government was already under pressure from the Liberal Party which was seeking to establish of a register of MPs' interests as well as initiate a wider inquiry.[12]

In some respects, Maudling's culpability or otherwise is a somewhat sterile debate although it does establish some context whereby the question of corruption came into the public domain and how it was perceived. The Poulson case was remarkable for the fact that it attracted vast media attention and that attention was also sustained over a long period. The original report about Poulson's bankruptcy was made by Raymond Fitzwalter in the *Bradford Telegraph and Argus* on 19 April 1970. The story was then picked up by Paul Foot who wrote a substantial article – 'The Slicker of Wakefield' – in his Footnotes column in *Private Eye* two weeks later.[13] Founded in 1961, *Private Eye* was an example of the new type of media. Its openly polemical and lampooning style caught the public imagination. It looked like a student magazine, and along with other magazines, its scurrilous and subversive output was reminiscent of the eighteenth-century caricaturists, Gillray and Rowlandson. In Foot's column, the suspects, apart from Poulson, were 'Desperate Dan' (T. Dan Smith) and 'Reckless Reggie' (Reginald Maudling). Poulson's network secured work throughout England, principally in Yorkshire and the north-east but also in London, the home counties as well as in Scotland. The case was then taken up by the national press, and once the corruption trial commenced, *The Times'* formerly specialised law reports now became major news items of popular interest. Not since the Belcher case and the Lynskey Tribunal in 1948–49 had a corruption case received so much attention. The popular press also had a field day with the cartoonists such as Stan McMurtry in the *Daily Mail* and Raymond Jackson as 'Jak' capturing the incredulity that their readerships felt.[14] Further, radio and television brought a new dimension to the exposure of political corruption, and Granada TV's *World in Action* was in the vanguard of this movement. In fact, Raymond Fitzwalter was to move to the Granada network bringing with him his investigative skills which were put to such good effect in the Gozo programme. *World in Action* had already pushed the boundaries when its first attempt to expose Poulson with its programme 'The friends and influence of John Poulson' was banned by the Independent Broadcasting Authority (IBA), presumably on the grounds that it amounted to trial by television and might have amounted to contempt. The action of the IBA provoked a strike of television technicians, and the following week viewers were faced with a blank screen when they turned on expecting *World in Action*. 'Shock night for TV millions' was the *Daily Mirror* headline.[15] Eventually, a compromise was struck and the *World in Action* programme was shown as 'The rise and fall of John Poulson' on 30 April 1973. The exposure of political figures was discomfiting to the political class, but it was welcomed by the police. Robert Mark, Commissioner of the Metropolitan Police, went out of his way to acknowledge the value of such programmes as *Nationwide* and *Midweek* (BBC) and *This Week*, *Today* and of course *World in Action* (ITV). In his annual reports throughout the mid-1970s, he cited the Poulson case every year for four consecutive years. The case had consumed vast investigative resources, but its significance impressed Mark to the point that he singled out the work of the Scotland Yard Press Force Bureau which he claimed had handled 10,000 specific news items and 120,000 telephone calls in 1972–73. He cited particular subjects that were matters of regular enquiry, and these included 'bombings in the London area, subversive activities and the Poulson case'.[16] In 1974, he was at pains to point out the demands that were being made on the Metropolitan Police citing the reappearance of Ronald Biggs, the attempted kidnapping of Princess Anne, the Millhench case and the search for Lord Lucan as well as Poulson and the disorders in Red Lion Square. Mark was an astute Commissioner and was adept at securing increased resources, but nevertheless his regular repetition of the significance of the case is telling. The increasingly interactive relationship between the press and the police was also recognised by the Salmon Commission. One of its members, Audrey Ward-Jackson observed that 'the police take the view that it is no part of their duties to seek out evidence of malpractice but only to start enquiries after information indicating malpractice has been provided to them'.[17]

The role of the press and other media in understanding the Poulson case cannot be minimised, and press revelation was a problem that the political class at this time probably failed to control. Moreover, it demonstrated modernity in that traditional codes of conduct were put to the test and exposed by the glare of new technologies such as television. The final abolition of newspaper print rationing in 1957 had already caused newspapers to expand in size. The need for even higher advertising revenues prompted a fierce circulation war between the popular dailies in which scandal, including corruption, was a central component of newspapers. The attitude of newspaper owners such as Cecil King signified a new approach and a stance that was anti-establishment. In an interview with Anthony Sampson in 1964, King expressed a not uncommon sentiment:

> I've never been a socialist. I'm anti-Tory, because I think the establishment is corrupt and incompetent; in the last thirteen years they have bungled nearly everything. By corruption I don't mean financial bribes; I mean appointing an old school friend to public office when you know he's not the best man- which is just as serious in its way ....[18]

The views of the great newspaper magnate would seem to have been in tune with those working-class men interviewed by Richard Hoggart for his *Uses of Literacy*. Further, the new genre of investigative journalism championed by Harold Evans at *The Sunday Times* brought a cutting edge to the Sunday broadsheets too. Evans had also worked in the north of England for the *Manchester Evening News* as a junior reporter and later for *The Northern Echo* as editor. So he was well versed in the politics of the north of England. The Poulson case is especially important because it raised the question of press freedom when publishing legal proceedings without risking contempt.

Additionally, the examination of Poulson and some of his replies were regarded as 'highly defamatory of certain individuals some of whom are well-known public men'.[19] MPs who also practised journalism were particularly likely to find themselves compromised. Thus, Joe Ashton, Labour MP for Bassetlaw and writer for the *Sheffield Star* and the *Labour Weekly*, found himself before the Committee of Privileges because of articles that he had written in both papers in April 1974. Ashton had since 1970 been actively committed to a campaign to introduce a register of interests for MPs, and he was willing to make his case in the press, on television and on radio. It was his venture into radio and his encounter with the disarmingly benign Jimmy Young that trapped him. Introducing his daytime show on 26 April 1974, Young said:

> He [Ashton] lists such things as phoney charities, lush trips and the PR game [and] it's quite easy to hire an MP, shall we say to pay a fee.

The format of the programme with a telephone link to BBC's Sheffield studio wrong-footed Ashton and when pressed by Young on the numbers of MPs involved Ashton replied:

> no more than half a dozen or so ... it doesn't do any real harm until it suddenly appears in the headlines, you know, Poulson or somebody such as that is in a bankruptcy case and the next thing you know, wham, there's big headlines, lush trips abroad or this sort of thing which does the parties tremendous damage, particularly if there's a by-election pending.

When Ashton was quizzed by the Privileges Committee, he admitted he had been caught off guard, but perhaps he had missed the point when he told his inquisitors that the Jimmy Young Show was only a 'lightweight housewives' gossip programme'. Perhaps Ashton was off-air when Jimmy Young rounded off with the *coup de grace*:

> So, that was Joe Ashton, Labour MP, as I say, in our BBC Sheffield studio and he was telling us how MPs make money 'on the side'. And I have no doubt you will have your own views on that.

The final sentence was the invitation to the phone-in, a relatively new form of media–audience interaction. Ashton was admonished by the Privileges Committee as his remarks were construed as allegations against unidentified members, 'thereby enabling suspicion to fall on innocent and guilty alike'.[20] The preservation of honour and reputation was the prime motive of the Privileges Committee.

How can we explain the Poulson case? It merits an exploration of a number of broad areas including changes in the ethical environment and, secondly, changes in the patterns of spending since these provided a new ambition for conspicuous consumption which attracted all the transgressors that we encounter in the Poulson network. Last there will be some observation about the role of political techniques especially as practised by T. Dan Smith. The shifts that had taken place in the ethical environment can be traced to the Second World War. All three of these developments were indicative of a broader process of modernisation. Although the workings of the ethical environment can be strangely hidden, they impinge upon practical reasoning informing notions of duty. It can shape emotional responses such as pride and shame and what we might consider our due or just dessert.[21] This last notion has clearly affected the behaviour of the corrupt and those who allowed themselves to be corrupted. Thus, Vivian Baker, Poulson's accountant, recalled a meeting between Poulson and an officer from the Inland Revenue:

> [The taxman] smiled tolerantly and inferred in a kindly way that Poulson could not do what he was proposing. But Poulson took this to be a nod and a wink. The truth was that Poulson thought the law was made for other people.[22]

The Salmon Commissioners recognised the issue of just reward. Thus, Audrey Ward-Jackson in her minority report observed that the local authority committee chairman 'may find himself sniped at by the media and despised by the public as a featherer of his own nest, while he himself believes that he is being inadequately rewarded for what he is doing'. His modest expenses were markedly inferior to the salary of the full-time official. T. Dan Smith certainly believed that some kind of reward was his due. In a BBC interview, he complained, 'People like me are expected to work full-time, without salaries, without staff, or even postage stamps'.[23] The ethical environment could also of course be codified in law which provide the parameters for standards of behaviour. It might be popularly assumed that the 1960s was the watershed in this respect as it is often portrayed as a decade that heralded a new permissiveness.[24] More likely, these shifts began in the 1940s. Additionally, our three transgressors – Poulson, Smith and Maudling – were probably untouched by the new permissiveness of the 1960s. They were all of an older generation born within a seven-year span between 1910 and 1917. They reached a formative stage in their business and political careers between 1935 and 1950. All three made good in the War. Poulson was unable to perform military service for medical reasons but took advantage of wartime conditions to make good. In *The Price*, he observed that his experience in Birmingham during the war showed him that businessmen were 'sliding around rigid wartime rules' and that councillors and civil servants colluded in these activities: 'In wartime it was not always expedient to bring their wily developers to book for such misdemeanours'.[25] Interestingly, Poulson's perception of what was acceptable behaviour showed greater latitude because it was wartime. When the War was over, Poulson was well placed to expand his range of business contacts as well as penetrate the thicket of rules and regulations that governed building plans in the public sector. Smith was a conscientious objector and was active in left-wing politics in Newcastle during the war and organised the Tyneside apprentices' strike in 1944. He became active in the international socialists movement and the International Friendship League where he met Ted Short. He was also active in the Peace Pledge Union. Thus, by the end of the War, he had established a political platform that secured him a place on Newcastle City Council in 1950. Smith had set up his own signwriting and painting and decorating business in 1937, and presumably he had sustained it during the War. In 1945, he opened a café near the shipyards but then went in to partnership in a decorating business. By 1957, he had businesses in Stockton, York, Durham and Newcastle, and by 1962 his company had regular contract work with the City Council.[26] Newcastle politics also had a reputation for graft, and in 1944, Arthur Morrison had ordered a Tribunal of Inquiry to investigate the activities of Councillor Richard Embleton. Smith would have been aware of Embleton's exploits and seemed to have adopted a similar approach. He was a charismatic but tough politician who believed that rules were there to be broken. By 1958, when Labour gained control of Newcastle City Council, Smith became chairman of the housing committee. He had captured the council and subdued it to his will. The *Newcastle Journal* in its obituary in 1993 characterised him as follows:

> An abrasive and an often ruthless town hall politician who had an intimidating physical presence and a booming voice which didn't brook argument. He could rule a committee room with a rod of iron. He could strike the fear of God into city hall officials.[27]

In his evidence to the Salmon Commission, Smith stated: 'The people ought to have better housing, fine city centres, first class recreational facilities ... and if the ordinary processes of government do not provide these, then the ordinary processes of government must be stretched and bent until they do so'.[28] Maudling too had a good War. He was rejected for active military service on grounds of poor eyesight but then secured a position first in RAF intelligence and later as private secretary to Archibald Sinclair, the Secretary of State for Air. At the end of the War, he glided effortlessly into the Conservative Party's Research Department and was also able to avoid repaying his Harmsworth research scholarship of £300 to the Middle Temple even though he abandoned his career in the law.[29] He was elected as the Conservative MP for Barnett in 1950. His career path was almost like that of a modern-day professional politician – university, political research, MP and cabinet minister. He cultivated an effortless and languid style. Like Poulson and Smith, he was not afraid to cut corners especially if he could sustain his expensive lifestyle. Indeed, apart from his association with Poulson, he struck up other questionable partnerships – the Real Estate Fund of America based in Bermuda – and he also became a consultant for the Peachey Corporation of Sir Eric Miller who had misused the Corporation's funds and committed suicide in 1977.

All three – Poulson, Maudling and Smith – were opportunists. Maudling and Smith were career politicians[30] albeit at different ends of the ideological spectrum. All three were transgressors in their approach and showed scant regard for due process. Their behaviours were shaped by the new patterns of consumer demand although perhaps Maudling's was shaped by the more traditional style of the patrician. Additionally, his wife's ambition for her charity – the Adeline Genee Theatre at East Grinstead as a kind of ballet version of Glyndebourne – was to draw Maudling and Poulson into doubtful territory. Poulson hoped that Maudling's name and reputation would promote his business and his readiness to support the Adeline Genee charity would secure a knighthood or some other honour. Poulson was to be disappointed as Maudling proved indolent and ineffective. Nevertheless, it was their determination to sustain a particular lifestyle that was the cement that linked them. Poulson's own house – Manasseh – was a symbol of the parvenu: 'To this day, I can pinpoint the exact spot on the Great North Road where he pulled up the Rolls and said, "Cynthia, I'm bankrupt"'.[31] Smith and his wife Ada loved overseas trips especially if Poulson paid for them although Smith could always disguise this luxury in the name of progress: 'My wife and I set off for Scandinavia on our own initiative, without asking the city to sponsor us or bless our visitation. We went off on a pilgrimage to speak to Arne Jacobsen and to look at some of his ideas in housing and city centre work'.[32] Maudling and his wife Beryl loved to impress, and their house at Chester Square was a modern-day salon of entertainment, and Beryl wanted the accoutrements that she thought her husband's patrician life required:

> She wanted the good life and the bright lights, and Reggie was not strong enough to stand up to her ... She got insatiably greedy for the good things in life. There was constant pressure at home for money, for something more. She never let up.[33]

The patterns of the new consumerism had certainly snared Poulson and Smith. Cynthia Poulson's role was, as she said, 'to grace his home'. Smith was attracted to the world of celebrity and wanted to affect that lifestyle:

> One of the happier perks was a reception we had at 10 Downing Street, where we met a host of sportsmen. As a follow-up to that I wrote an allegedly humorous article for *Punch* with lots of name dropping and casual references to Henry Cooper and Georgie Best and their ilk. What genuinely intrigued me in meeting these sportsmen was their absorption in leisure rather than work.[34]

The patterns of consumer demand that characterised the period from the late 1950s have been much written about.[35] However, for Poulson the gravy train was drying up as the fluctuations in the cycle of investment for the British construction industry began to contract. Maudling, too, found that his income as a backbencher after 1972 was insufficient to sustain his wife's rapacious consumption of his income. He sought alternative sources of income as consultant, journalist and company director. This was a 'grey' area of potential corruption but which now probably seems 'blacker' because of Maudling's high status. It was not an unusual path for the career politician but the relationships with Poulson and Peachey Properties showed bad judgement.

The question of political techniques practised by Dan Smith raises important questions for the matter of corruption. It is important to examine the use of public relations as a process and Smith's own public relations companies. In Smith's hands, public relations was a malign influence. Employing local authority councillors as consultants with fees and commissions whilst those same councillors voted through housing schemes and city centre redevelopment projects was contrary to the requirements of the 1933 Local Government regulations which required councillors to declare their interests. The fallout of the Poulson trials included the discrediting of the nascent public relations industry. Public relations had developed in America, and the Institute of Public Relations was founded in Britain in 1948, and public relations companies gave evidence to Lord Salmon's Commission. Public relations entailed the management of public opinion and the building of relations between institutions and their publics or client groups. Public relations as projected by government took on a special paradigm in light of a planned economy post-1945. 'The new profession of the planner, the allocator of scarce resources, spread through government departments and local authorities'.[36] J.H. Brebner who had a distinguished career in the Post Office in the 1920s and 1930s became a key figure in the Ministry of Information during the Second World War and in 1949 published his *Public Relations and Publicity*. In Newcastle, T. Dan Smith began to realise the potential of public relations and established T. Dan Smith Associates and a series of other companies. The potential of public relations in the area of planning and redevelopment was also promoted by experts such as Wilfred Burns who had been Senior Planner in Coventry and in Newcastle:

> By far the most important initial effort in a redevelopment scheme is made perhaps by a few officers and the chairman of the appropriate committee in securing the enthusiasm among the elected representatives forming the committee responsible for the work ...[37]

Burns set out the principles of public relations in so far as they were related to urban redevelopment in the 1960s. It involved the press, building relations with potential client groups, such as prospective council house tenants, providing a plan for consultation, photographs and importantly models of the future development:

> Throughout all the proceedings, however, if the press are treated as friends in the business of improving the town, rather than enemies of truth or local government and therefore to be avoided at all costs, better public relations can be expected.[38]

Smith appreciated the potential of such an approach and assiduously recruited councillors and local journalists to his public relations organisations. These included Maurice Byrne a councillor in Poulson's home town of Pontefract and Jack Ramsey and Thomas Bergman of JKT Public Relations with whom Smith had close links. At the same time, Smith became a frontman for the Scottish building firm, Crudens. By such means, Smith was able to circumvent Section 76 of the 1933 Local Government Act which required councillors to declare their interests when speaking or voting on planning matters. Smith had also secretly employed Michael Ward, a TUC official, who had a liaison role for local government and who proved 'indispensable' to Smith and Poulson.[39] By such means, Smith was able to obscure the frontier between probity and corruption. Smith attempted to save face by claiming that he had always acted in good faith but that it was through Poulson's actions that he became associated, wrongly, with a 'sinister and clandestine grouping'. Smith persisted with this line even when he was in Leyhill prison claiming that he had no contact with Poulson after September 1968 and therefore that it was 'unfair to infer that[he] was the principal associate'.[40] Smith's protestations of innocence held no sway, and the popular press reported that Smith's public relations companies provided cover for councillors, 'without declaring their interests to use their influence on Mr Poulson's behalf'.[41] Smith's malign presence was neatly captured by Richard West, writing in *The Spectator* in 1976:

> Thanks to the secrecy imposed by the PROs [Public Relations Officers] Birmingham has been knocked down and plundered by its incompetent and in some cases corrupt rulers. The country's leading public relations expert, T. Dan Smith, not only got an account for the Northern Labour Party but managed to keep this secret for more than a year … Public relations men are useful to businesses that want to wreck the country's environment[42]

Smith's tactics were not always accepted. In Blyth, the local MP, Eddie Milne, was deeply suspicious of Smith and attempted to introduce a private member's bill to register the clients of public relations companies. He was unsuccessful and was deselected by his local constituency association.[43] We should not, however, overemphasise Smith's role or indeed the role of councillors. There were many other participants: trade union officials employed at national and regional levels were highly influential especially if they had links with the construction industry. Local authority clerks of works who were union men could also collude with building contractors, and this was a vital relationship since the degree of latitude on passing the standard of work done could impact upon profit margins. These actors also operated within a set of circumstances that were out of their control but could also shape behaviour. The complex web of land use and planning laws, local authority approaches to development control and tolerance or otherwise of changes of use from residential use to office use all played their part. Additionally, contracts for housing construction brought in a variety of contractors to provide related road and sewer contracts. Speculative builders who had already bought land which a local authority later sought to buy for a housing estate, for example, could exploit their position to considerable advantage especially if they had contacts with particular councillors or officers who were unscrupulous. Builders, architects and civil engineering partnerships constituted a powerful network of influence where the potential for corrupt transactions was ever present. Other professionals such as solicitors, accountants and surveyors could also play key roles in this web of corruption. Smith's own insights are revealing: the 'ring around the architect, sub-contractors, contractors, other professions, suppliers all of them form a lobby for "their" scheme [and] no declarable interests are involved'.[44]

The Poulson corruption case was not merely a scandalous episode. It has also been claimed that Harold Wilson's conduct was questionable and his relationship with Joseph Kagan became a matter of satirical ridicule. It was of critical significance as it revealed a complex set of relationships between national and local politicians as well as the world of business, especially the construction industry which was so important to deindustrialising Britain. The Poulson–Smith affair represented then a new paradigm that corruption occurs in periods of modernisation or at least transition. It is practised by the upwardly mobile who are attracted to 'conspicuous consumption' and who rationalise rule breaking as a legitimate means of extracting some reward as recompense for their 'good' works.

Ultimately, the corruptions of Poulson and Smith discredited local government to an enormous degree so much so that after 1979 with the governments of Margaret Thatcher, local authorities were not to be trusted with redevelopment projects. They were replaced with Development Corporations and other quangos which would by the 1990s be scrutinised by the Nolan Commission. Poulson was important too because of public reaction and the nature of contemporary debate. Further, the broader economic and political environment that fuelled the building boom of the 1960s from which Poulson profited must also be understood as should the nature of power in the urban political environment in 1950s and 1960s Britain. Salmon gives us an initial glimpse of the affair, but it had little impact and was limited as an investigative instrument as it was powerless to compel witnesses to give evidence, its proceedings were slow, and many of the witnesses were employed by public bodies or represented them as elected figures and they may not have been entirely frank.

Let us begin with the contemporary debate about corruption in local, specifically, urban politics. The Poulson affair attracted attention because contemporaries thought it a rare and therefore a shocking occurrence.[45] The vehement reaction of the Judge when passing sentence was indicative of this shock and apparent rarity. Corruption may be 'context dependent' but it certainly implies a departure from expected standards of behaviour and the value system that those standards imply. Specifically, there was a conflict of values as articulated by the national elite – judges, civil servants, churchmen and some cabinet ministers – who expected high-minded public duty rather than the grubby ethic apparently prevalent in local government. Above all it was the naked venality of Poulson's bribes that dismayed so profoundly. The atmosphere of corruption seemed all pervasive, and it was not only Reginald Maudling who exemplified questionable integrity. Earlier, Ernest Marples, Minister for Transport in MacMillan's government from 1959 to 1964, also portrayed a new go-getting type. He was the founder of the civil engineering company Marples Ridgway which secured the contract for the Hammersmith Flyover in the late 1950s.[46] Marples coincidentally became Minister for Transport in 1959. It was sufficient for Marples to make a personal statement to the House of Commons which the Speaker accepted, adding that the issue was not open to debate[47] as the honour of MPs was assumed unless proved otherwise. This had not applied to local alderman and councillors who had been required to declare their interests since the Local Government Act 1933. Significantly, Poulson's corruptions were uncovered at a time when the increased scope of government management of the economy generally, and building and planning specifically, had never been greater. Poulson's activities entailed numerous offences against the Corruption Acts. To Lord Salmon's commissioners, the Poulson case made them acutely aware of the problem of standards in public life and their tension with practices in the private sector. The structure of urban politics in the north of England and Smith's use of public relations techniques all highlighted the dangers when large public building contracts were at stake.

The complex nature of local planning reveals the limiting quality of legal definition in respect of corruption. Poulson's experience in Yorkshire during the Second World War had taught him that once a building contract had been granted, then the local authority, Knottingley Urban District Council in Poulson's career, was likely to retain the same architects and builders for subsequent contracts. So what was the price to be paid to secure repeat business? He sometimes overpriced contracts providing a completion date that he knew he could beat. Completing under budget and on time could set the scene for further work. Once these tactics had worked, it was then a small step to disperse the potential surpluses in later contracts in the form of bribes, gifts, holidays and even home improvements for councillors. Poulson said that he had been duped by T. Dan Smith, but he recognised that Smith 'enjoyed favours', and so after Smith's heart attack in 1964, Poulson paid for a holiday of convalescence. Subsequently, he paid for many holidays for other associates claiming that they were 'restorative' for those working in the demanding and pressurised world of business. He accepted though that his association with Smith was 'the crux of [his] own downfall'[48] and that it was the *Private Eye* campaign against Reginald Maudling that was ultimately so damaging. Poulson had also claimed in the witness box when cross-examined by Muir Hunter QC that Harry Vincent, the Chief Executive of Bovis, had made funds available to pay for Smith's services.[49] What are we to make of all this? Should we be prepared to consider the proposition that corruption was more widespread than Salmon's Report admitted? Poulson's defence at his trial may appear simply to be disingenuous: 'I have been brought up that it is a greater pleasure to give than to receive'.[50] He also claimed, 'I have squandered money on people I thought were my friends. They conned me. I did not realise what an old twit I had been until I heard some of the evidence here'.[51]

Journalists and historians alike have presented Poulson's corruption as illegal and immoral using the case as emblematic of wider moral turpitude. Corruption then is seen in terms of binary opposites: good–wicked and honest–dishonest.[52] In accounts of developing and especially postcolonial societies, corruption has been presented as an instance of the rational bureaucratic state in conflict with an older more traditional even patrimonial, tribal, clannish culture.[53] Weberian concepts that link modernisation – the imposition of rational legality on traditional cultural practices – may not sit well with Poulson's behaviour,[54] but in private business, the culture gifts in the form of Christmas cheer, entertainment and holidays were common. So, in his autobiography Poulson, extolling his self-made-man credentials, refers to his grandfather who had established a successful pottery business at Ferrybridge, Yorkshire, in the nineteenth century. His grandfather employed a large number of people and was 'open handed and generous to an extreme and in a way which was far more acceptable in his day than it was to be in mine'.[55] This might be regarded as a self-deception. However, none of those who benefited from Poulson's generosity had reported the matter. So was the protocol of 'giving' acceptable in the environment in which Poulson operated? Was Poulson so skilled as to allow those with whom he came in contact to regard their own rewards as legitimate? By setting aside binary opposites, we could consider that many activities were often regarded by participants as normal. However, the conduct of the law and the discourse of politicians adopted the stark counterpoint of right or wrong, good or wicked. The establishment view as articulated by judges and clergymen saw corrupt behaviour as a betrayal of the Lockean virtue of trust. Poulson, though, understood that political decisions, such as a planning consent, were shaped by human partiality. As such, that partiality could be bought by flattery and obsequiousness and also by holidays, suits, lunches and home improvements. There is though a close but contradictory relationship between these apparently polarised positions bordering on furtive fascination fuelled by gossip, rumour, conspiracy, innuendo and accusation.[56] Muir Hunter QC certainly exploited this when questioning Poulson at his trial suggesting that he was distributing favours. 'What friend gives a house to a friend?' asked Peter Taylor QC prosecuting George Pottinger, the senior Scottish Office civil servant. 'He was living in a Poulson house, driving a Poulson car, wearing Poulson suits, and travelling on Poulson expenses'.[57] The trial reports displayed particular glee in the revelations of Poulson's gifts, but perhaps Poulson's corruptions were not especially unusual. Between 1964 and 1968, there were 757 cases of corruption brought before Magistrates' Courts, and 89 were committed for trial in Crown Court, of which seventy-nine were found guilty. These included Poulson and the twenty other people caught up in his schemes. Poulson's case accounts for slightly more than a tenth of all the cases. Overall, however, the twenty-one convictions involved in the Poulson case represent less than three per cent of all the cases proceeded against in both the Magistrates and Crown Courts. So, in some respects, public alarm was conceivably disproportionate to legal reality. Indeed, the eighty-nine cases taken to Crown Court between 1964 and 1978 were less than the number of cases indicted in the earlier periods 1904–10 and 1926–28 (see Appendix). There was nonetheless sufficient to speculate that the extent of corruption in 1950s and 1960s Britain was greater than Salmon's Report acknowledged despite press coverage and that television had brought the case into people's homes in a new and dramatic way.[58]

Poulson's case was perhaps just another instance of wrongdoing with only the nature of its revelation being something new and extraordinary. Indeed, there has been a tradition which portrayed municipal government in the late Victorian and Edwardian period as symbolic of a 'golden age' when high-minded probity apparently prevailed.[59] However, in Salford in 1887, the corporation's gas manager attempted to bribe a local coal contractor. The coal contractor was lauded in the press as a hero who had struck a 'blow for public and commercial ethics'.[60] A case of particular audacity was that of an accountant clerk to Wolverhampton's education committee who defrauded the corporation of over £84,000 between 1905 and 1917.[61]

The sense of anxiety, however, that arose with the Poulson case was on a scale perhaps unprecedented. Corruption was something that happened in other countries or so politicians schooled in Britain's imperial past liked to imagine, and therefore it was all the more shocking when it was present here. MPs were sensitive to the revelatory nature of the case, but politicians also played the same game as the press concentrating on the more lurid implications of the scandal. Thus, David Steel the Liberal Party Chief Whip addressed his constituents in Hawick: 'We have been quick in the past to crack down on politicians guilty of some sexual peccadillo. Far more corrupting of a nation's morality is the misuse by politicians and public officials of their positions for private gain'. It was a good issue for the Liberals to dwell on, and Steel showed little restraint:

> Financial corruption is common place in the public life of many countries, not just Africa, Asia, or South America but also in Europe and even the United States … In Britain it is rare [but] if we are not to drag ourselves to the status of banana republic the Government must act to remove any possibility of improper or personal gain on the part of those holding high office.[62]

In a more measured way though, the Salmon Commission recognised that there were different standards of behaviour that applied in public life to those which might prevail in private business. The commissioners were disappointed that the scope of their inquiry excluded private business but observed that 'the ethics of society at large must have a bearing on the standards observed in the public sector'.[63] Lord Houghton believed the case was so shocking it merited an investigation into the standards of conduct in commercial and industrial life lamenting that this 'mischief mainly lies at the meeting points along the boundary between public service and private interests'.[64] With Poulson, this concerned the arrangements that prevailed between the construction industry, civil engineering, the planning process and public bodies because post-war governments had built a consensus around the reconstruction of Britain's urban fabric. The Macmillan government had used housebuilding statistics skilfully to appeal to the electorate.[65] So the period from 1950 to 1969 was a bonanza for building council houses and redeveloping town centres, hospitals, office blocks, schools and public baths. Between 1961 and 1970, there were 3.2 million houses built in England and Wales and 685,000 slums demolished. This was more than two times higher than the building that had taken place between 1938 and 1950 and twenty-six per cent higher than the volume built in 1951–60.[66] Much of Britain's housing stock was decrepit encouraging wholesale demolition with the result that over a million houses were demolished between 1951 and 1970 often replaced by high-rise blocks built quickly and cheaply using the Skarne and similar construction systems. Conservative governments of the 1950s relaxed the system of licences for granting planning approval, and this was against a background of deindustrialisation where building and construction was regarded as a source of economic growth. At local level, problems of new building and development were expedited, from the politicians' standpoint, by negotiation rather than competitive tendering. Poulson was especially adept in this environment. His business was large and its impact on post-war urban Britain was considerable with over 240 planned projects. Indeed, he was responsible for designing a range of urban structures from schools and colleges; hospitals; swimming baths; shops and town centre developments; industrial buildings; office blocks; National Coal Board (NCB) headquarters, colliery buildings and offices for gas companies; civic buildings including town council buildings and libraries; and railway stations. He also designed domestic dwellings including individual bespoke structures for private clients as well as local authority housing estates and specialist provision for pensioners in the form of sheltered housing schemes. Lastly, there were plans and designs for working men's clubs, sports complexes and a tourist centre.[67] There were town centre redevelopment plans for Felling in Tyne and Wear, Mexborough in Yorkshire and Southport in Lancashire. His work had particular geographical concentrations: over 170 commissions in Yorkshire with Bradford, Pontefract–Knottingley, Leeds, Sheffield and Wakefield accounting for half of all the Yorkshire plans. The Stockton-on-Tees and Middlesbrough–Hartlepool area accounted for nineteen commissions, and Darlington, Durham, Consett, Newcastle and Sunderland account for the majority of the rest. There was work elsewhere and his mark can be found all over Britain. This should be set alongside the fact that the construction market in the public sector was dominated by just seven companies – Wimpy, Concrete, Laing, Wates, Taylor Woodrow, Camus and Crudens – and Poulson had links with at least four. Finally, Poulson as an architect was not alone in resorting to corrupt practice. Patrick Dunleavy's work amply demonstrates these matters in Birmingham, where Alan Maudsley, the city's chief architect 1966–73, dispensed considerable patronage over negotiated contracts and he gave out, in return for payments, work to a small local architectural firm – Ebery and Sharp – that transformed its business.[68]

The structure of Poulson's businesses was innovative combining numerous functions – architectural planning together with engineering – which enabled him to plan in many diverse settings. At its peak, his companies employed 750 staff with offices in Pontefract, his original base, but also in London, Middlesbrough, Newcastle, Edinburgh, Beirut and Lagos. Poulson's business activity was vulnerable to the changes of tempo in the overall economy which was in turn subject to the calibrations of the government. The construction industry was highly sensitive to these changes, and it was the slowdown in building activity that caused Poulson's bankruptcy. Increasingly, he looked overseas and this was why he thought Reginald Maudling's status as a former cabinet minister would open doors, but from 1969 onwards, the construction industry moved in to recession, and this was to prove so critical in Poulson's downfall. In January 1970, John Silkin, Minister for Housing, met with construction industry leaders who were seeking some mitigation from the effects of the credit squeeze, the Selective Employment Tax and dwindling demand.[69] Although government was sympathetic to the construction industry, the budget measures of April 1970 were too little too late. Further, although the raising of the school leaving age was expected to boost the local authority schools' building programme, it was too late for Poulson. Indeed, the rate of bankruptcies reported had almost doubled between 1964 and 1970, and construction companies were amongst the biggest losers. Architectural commissions were also a function of planning and anticipated building activity, and Poulson's own housebuilding plans had reached their peak in 1965, and although he had a diverse portfolio, his overall planned commissions in Britain had shrunk by more than forty per cent between 1969 and 1971.

Poulson had been able to profit from the building boom because he was already well placed. Central government's decision to make the construction industry the engine of economic growth was undoubtedly decisive. Poulson, T. Dan Smith and Alan Maudsley profited from these circumstances as did property developers such as Sir Charles Clore and Jack Cotton.[70] However, the demand for public building projects was essentially inelastic, and so when the economy moved into recession, Poulson looked overseas from Angola to the United Arab Emirates. The Poulson affair revealed the nature of power in post-1950s Britain at least until the break-up of the post-war consensus after 1979. The programme of reconstruction was an ideal vehicle for central government to direct resources through local authorities in the name of social justice and economic recovery. The use of block grants-in-aid of the rates and regional economic development councils was seemingly achieving utopian solutions to the problems that had blighted Britain in the 1930s and 1940s. Poulson's bribes though brought into question the efficacy of local government as the tool for such a grand purpose. The convergence of the lessons of the Salmon Commission and the Redcliffe-Maud Report on local government helped to create a new view that the existing urban government structure was ill-suited to the management and direction of large infrastructural projects. Local councillors were ill-equipped to deal with such tasks, and so the tendency for central government to adopt *dirigiste* solutions became stronger still. The affair also revealed that the nature of power was transactional and that the relationships it structured were asymmetrical. In this sense, Poulson was probably located at an intermediate to low point in the hierarchy of power. He was dependent on the patronage of T. Dan Smith or was clutching at the cachet that Reginald Maudling's name might lend to his business prospectus. Paying for that patronage or that social association was indicative of Poulson's dependency on others. Further, the fallout from the case revealed complex relationships between ministers, civil servants, public officials and local councillors. The leading executives of large construction companies certainly had more leverage than Poulson as only a licentiate member of that gentlemanly organisation, the Royal Institute of British Architects. Poulson's brazen audacity compromised the assumed gentlemanly conduct of politics that had evolved from the construction of the liberal state since 1832. The rationality of that state had been founded on the principle of 'voluntary self-restraint'.[71] The conduct of Poulson, Smith, Maudsley and Maudling flew in the face of that principle. It suggested that politicians – especially local government politicians – were unable to manage their own ethical boundaries. Consequently, public distrust of politicians grew. Indeed, a public opinion survey published in 1973 suggested that as many as four out of every ten voters agreed with the proposition that 'many local councillors get a dishonest financial advantage from being on the council'.[72] The ramifications of this loss of trust as well as a lack of competence were not instantly apparent, but they were to become so after 1979 when Margaret Thatcher's governments resolved not only to break local government[73] but also to create new organisational instruments – Corporations and Housing Trusts, for example – to deliver urban redevelopment projects. Moreover, there was after 1979 a growing hostility towards local, particularly urban, government and a mountain of legislation eroded its powers. New auditing arrangements, curbs on tax-raising and spending powers, starving it of funds,[74] and outsourcing municipal government services all came in to play. This was as much politically motivated as anything else, but the Poulson affair had done much to sully the reputation of local government. It should then be central in an examination of the processes which caused the marginalisation of urban government which went on apace after 1979. Salmon had demonstrated the vulnerability of local government institutions and the shortcomings of its office holders when large building projects were at stake. Poulson's own business experience and his bankruptcy was an illustration of the vulnerability of the construction industry and architectural businesses to national government's management of the economy. The affair then was crucial in dissolving the post-1950 consensus around urban planning, economic management and the powers of local government which went on apace after 1979. Undoubtedly, it contributed to the growing cynicism about politics, and the affair reveals neatly the interplay between journalists and the media on the one hand and politicians, national and local, on the other. Poulson's corruptions revealed changing moralities, the dangers of the business cycles of the construction industry and the nature of political power in urban Britain.

It also stereotyped the north of England as a place apart from the rest of the nation. Such an image was also fostered by journalists and commentators. For instance, Graham Turner, the BBC's economics correspondent, had like Dickens and Orwell before him, chosen to travel north in the 1960s. He found a region whose people expressed a fierce identity fostered by a sense of solidarity and historic exploitation. The resultant bitterness was directed against London and the south of England. The Hunger March and the legacy of the 1930s reinforced a powerful sense of grievance. It was this kind of consciousness that T. Dan Smith exploited so effectively. He was the city boss, *par excellence*, and working-class leaders like Smith and Cunningham were 'Mr Newcastle' and 'Mr Felling', respectively. Locals paid 'homage, to both elected and paid officials [and it was] commonplace for the area and the men themselves to be perfectly frank about the extent of their influence [as] they seem[ed] to be virtually tribal chiefs appointed for life'.[75] The esteem in which they were held led them to believe that they were invincible. They became intoxicated by their own power. Smith understood well the power structures of the towns and cities of the north. He knew the leading trade union officials and their influence over clerks of works in building contracts, and he was at ease too with professionals such as lawyers, accountants and surveyors. Between 1945 and 1967, Labour controlled Newcastle for sixteen years out of twenty-three, and Labour dominated the towns and cities of the north where Smith was able to secure contracts and commissions for Poulson. Smith's confidence and overriding certainty and his skilful use of public relations techniques were critical to the widespread nature of corrupt practice. Further, his apparent credibility in the eyes of Labour's national leadership gave him great leverage in power broking resources for the region. Corruption in the north-east then was a consequence of a belief in the unassailability of its leaders. The consequences were serious. Conservatives gained control of Newcastle in 1967, and Labour's heroic age ended. The age of civic virtue also closed after the Poulson trials, and the subsequent stagflation of the economy following the oil shocks of the early 1970s eroded the consensus of economic management that had prevailed since 1945 and of which local government had been a key partner.

Notes

1 Betjeman, J., 'The executive', *Collected Poems* (London: John Murry, 1979), p. 313.
2 Poulson, J., *The Price: The Autobiography of John Poulson, Architect* (London: Michael Joseph, 1981), p. 183.
3 Fitzwalter, R. and D. Taylor, *Web of Corruption: The Story of J.G.L. Poulson and T. Dan Smith* (London: Granada, 1981); Baston, L., *Reggie: The Life of Reginald Maudling* (Stroud: Sutton, 2004).
4 *The Times*, 2 May 1974, 3 May 1974.
5 *The Times*, 12 February 1974.
6 *The Times*, 4 January 1974.
7 Poulson, C., 'My generous, foolish husband', *Woman's Own*, 19 February 1977.
8 Poulson, *The Price*, p. 183.
9 *Poulson (a bankrupt) Re ex-parte Granada Television v. Maudling*, 2 All ER 1020 (1976) 1 WLR 1023, SOl JO734 (1976) from The Lexis Law Library, www.lexisnexis.co.uk visited on 13 April 2011.
10 *Ibid.*
11 NA, CAB 128/58/37, 13 July 1972.
12 NA, CAB 128/50/35, 6 July 1972.
13 Foot, P., 'The slicker of Wakefield', *Private Eye*, 24 April 1970.
14 McMurtry, S., *Daily Mail*, 27 September 1972 (Item 23156); and Jackson, R., *Evening Standard*, 1 May 1974 (Item 26142) from the British Cartoons Archive, www.cartoons.ac.uk, visited on 13 April 2011.
15 Quoted in Fitzwalter and Taylor, *Web of Corruption*.
16 See House of Commons Parliamentary Papers, *Reports of the Commissioner of Police for the Metropolis* (1974–75), Cmd., 6068; (1975–76), Cmd., 6496; (1976–77), Cmd., 6821.
17 *Royal Commission on Standards of Conduct in Public Life* (1976), Cmd., 6524, para. 8, p. 119.
18 Cecil King was Chairman of International Publishing Corporation and controlled the *Daily Mirror*, the *Sunday Mirror*, the *People* and the *Sun*; quoted by Sampson, A., *The Anatomy of Britain Today* (London: Hodder and Stoughton,1965), p. 142.
19 HCP, *Report of the Committee on Defamation* (1974–75), Cmd., 5909, para. 196, p. 50.
20 HCP, *First Report of the Committee of Privileges* (1974), HC, 228, p. xxvii.
21 Blackburn, S., *Ethics: A Very Short Introduction* (Oxford: Oxford University Press, 2001), 1; and Grayling, *Ideas That Matter* (2009), p. 173.
22 Quoted by Fitzwalter and Taylor, *Web of Corruption*, p. 165.
23 Quoted in Chibnall and Saunders, 'Worlds apart' (1977), pp. 138–54.
24 Marwick, *The Sixties* (1998); Booker, C., *The Neophiliacs: a study of the revolution in English life in the fifties and sixties* (London: Collins, 1969); Jarvis, *Conservative Governments* (2005).

25 Poulson, *The Price*, 24.
26 Smith, *An Autobiography* (1970), pp. 17–33; Fitzwalter and Taylor, *Web of Corruption*, pp. 39–40.
27 *Newcastle Journal*, 28 July 1993.
28 *Standards of Conduct* (1976), para. 9, p. 20.
29 Baston, *Reggie*, p. 31; and Shepherd, R., 'Maudling, Reginald 1917–1979', *Oxford Dictionary of National Biography*, www.oxforddnb.com, visited on 15 December 2009.
30 King, A., The rise of the career politician and its consequences', *British Journal of Political Science*, 11: 3 (1981), pp. 249–85.
31 Poulson, C., *Woman's Own*, 19 February 1977.
32 Smith, *An Autobiography*, p. 56.
33 Private interview quoted by Lewis Baston in *Reggie*, p. 265.
34 Smith, *An Autobiography*, p. 74.
35 Sandbrook, D., *Never Had It So Good: A History of Britain from Suez to the Beatles* (Little Brown, London, 2005).
36 Harrison, *Seeking* (2009), p. 43.
37 Burns, W., *New Towns for Old: The Technique of Urban Renewal* (London: Leonard Hill, 1963), p. 187.
38 Burns, *New Towns for Old*, p. 188.
39 NA, T. Dan Smith, Memorandum to Secretary of *Standards of Conduct in Public Life*, 16 September 1975. Ward would become later MP for Peterborough. H.O. 241/98.
40 NA, *Standards of Conduct in Public Life*, H.O. 241/98. T. Dan Smith Written Evidence C458647: Letter and memorandum to the secretary of the Commission, 22 July 1976.
41 *Daily Express*, 16 July 1976.
42 West, R., 'The PR Humbug', *The Spectator*, 16 October, 1976.
43 Milne, *No Shining Armour* (1976).
44 NA, *Standards of Conduct in Public Life*. HO 241/98 Secretary of the Commission interview with T. Dan Smith, Leyhill Prison, Evidence N0. 76, 16 September 1975.
45 Moore, J. and J. Smith, 'Corruption and urban governance', in Moore and Smith (eds.), *Corruption in Urban Politics*, p. 3.
46 *The Times*, 23 January 1960.
47 HC Debates, 28 January 1960, vol. 616, cc. 380–81.
48 Poulson, *The Price*, p. 69.
49 NA. H.O. 241/98, *Standards*, Background Paper No. 37: Laing and Bovis.
50 *Ibid.*
51 *Ibid.*
52 Nuijten and Anders, *Corruption and the Secret of the Law* (2007), pp. 1–24.
53 Huntington, S., *Political Order in Changing Societies* (New Haven: Yale University Press, 1969).
54 Huntington, *Political Order*; Weber, M., *Economy and Society: An Outline of Interpretative Sociology* (New York: Bedminster Press, 1968).
55 Poulson, *The Price*, p. 14.
56 Nuijten and Anders, *Corruption and the Secret of the Law*, pp. 1–24.
57 *The Times*, 2 February 1974.
58 'The rise and fall of John Poulson', *World in Action*, 30 April 1973.
59 Laski, et al., *Century of Municipal Progress*. For a valuable explanation, see Harrison, B., *Transformation of British Politics 1860–1995* (Oxford: Clarendon Press, 1996); Loughlin, M., *Half a Century of Municipal Decline: 1935–1985* (London: Allen and

Unwin, 1985); T. Byrne, *Local Government in Britain: Everyone's Guide to How It All Works* (London, Penguin, 1994).

60 Garrard, J., 'Scandals: a tentative overview', in Moore and Smith, *Corruption in Urban Politics*, p. 24.

61 Smith, J., 'Ingenious and daring': The Wolverhampton Council Fraud 1905–1917', in Moore and Smith, pp. 113–15.

62 *The Times*, 10 July 1972.

63 *Standards of Conduct*, para. 30, p. 10.

64 *Standards of Conduct* (1976), Lord Houghton's Addendum, para. 5, p. 121.

65 Dunleavy, P., *The Politics of Mass Housing 1945–1975: A Study of Corporate Power and Professional Influence in the Welfare State* (Oxford Clarendon Press: 1981); Ravetz, A., 'Housing the people', in Fyrth, J. (ed.), *Labour's Promised Land* (Lawrence and Wishart, 1995); and Larkham, P., 'Rebuilding the industrial town: wartime Wolverhampton', *Urban History*, 29: 3 (2002), pp. 388–409.

66 Halsey, A.H., *Twentieth Century British Social Trends*, 3rd edn (Basingstoke: Macmillan, 2000).

67 The tourist centre was at Aviemore in Scotland and owed much to Poulson's link with George Pottinger of the Scottish Office.

68 For a comprehensive examination of Birmingham's redevelopment and Maudsley's role, see Dunleavy, *Politics of Mass Housing*, pp. 292–301.

69 *The Times*, 12 February 1970.

70 Marriott, O., *Property Boom* (London: Hamish Hamilton, 1967).

71 Vincent, *Culture of Secrecy* (1998), p. 314.

72 *The Times*, 6 August 1973.

73 Gilmour, I., *Dancing with Dogma: Britain Under Thatcherism* (London: Simon and Schuster, 1992), pp. 143–6, pp. 212–20.

74 Baugh, 'Government grants' (1992), pp. 215–33.

75 Turner, G., *The North Country* (London: Eyre and Spottiswoode, 1967).

5　London corruption: the fall of the House of Porter

> It should be noted ... how easily men are corrupted, and in nature become transformed, however good they may be and however well brought up.
>
> Niccolo Machiavelli, *The Discourses* (1519)[1]

> My provisional view is that the council was involved in gerrymandering, which I am minded to find is a disgraceful and improper purpose and not a purpose for which a local authority may act.
>
> John Magill, District Auditor for the City of Westminster (1994)[2]

London's politics from 1963, when the London County Council (LCC) was abolished and replaced by the Greater London Council (GLC) until it too was wound up in 1986, were marked by confusion and overlapping responsibilities between the individual boroughs and the GLC itself. These circumstances produced the classic conditions of *immobilisme*. Ostensibly, the GLC was charged with determining the strategic development of the capital, and the individual boroughs were responsible for operational matters within their own boundaries. The GLC had authority for the Greater London Development Plan, whereas the individual London boroughs approved planning applications within their own boundaries. The division of obligations between the GLC and the boroughs for road and traffic management was equally blurred although from 1970 the GLC assumed the role of the Transport Planning Authority for London. In housing, there was again replication of duties especially after 1974 when the boroughs were encouraged to promote improvement areas and renovate older housing stock. However, the fact that the GLC had inherited a vast housing stock from the old LCC meant in effect there were again uncertain demarcation lines. Additionally, the GLC was to take charge of education in the inner London boroughs. For this purpose, a statutory committee, the Inner London Education Authority (ILEA), was set up, but the GLC had no responsibility for the outer London boroughs who all maintained their own education authority status.

London was also special because the politics of the nation and the affairs of the locality overlapped. London then became the stage upon which the dramatic struggle between a national government intent upon the transformation of local government and a new class of political activists who sought to defend local autonomy by means of a curious brand of politics which espoused individual rights and a whole range of 'causes' many of which seemed, to contemporaries on the right, unrelated to the concerns of local government. London, too, attracted the ambitious, many of whom used local government as a platform from which to launch a national career. It was easier to be noticed in London. Indeed, of the Labour MPs elected for London's constituencies in 2010, fifty-eight per cent had served as councillors in London boroughs having been elected there as early as 1973 and as late as 1994. For the Conservatives, forty-eight per cent of their London MPs elected in 2010 had served as councillors, or as members of the London Assembly or in one case a London MEP. The Conservative MP who was the earliest serving councillor had been elected in 1986 and the most recent in 2002. Those of more patrician backgrounds – titled families, the sons of plutocrats, membership of the Bullingdon Club and senior military career – could avoid the lacklustre business of local government. Arguably, the potential for corruption amongst career politicians who 'lived by politics' was always present: they were ambitious risk-takers and they believed they would always move on.

London's politics in this crucial period from 1965 to 1985 became fiercely ideological with Ken Livingstone, a skilful, articulate, self-publicist and the most able of the politicians of the new urban left, and Horace Cutler, an outspoken maverick on the new right. Cutler had served as Mayor of Harrow in 1958–59. The incorporation of Middlesex into the newly established GLC provided Cutler with a national platform. He became chairman of the GLC housing committee in 1967, and he became the most prominent advocate of the sale of council houses to aspirant working-class families. By the time the Conservatives lost their majority on the GLC, it had sold 16,000 council dwellings, a feat that owed much to Cutler. Livingstone and Cutler were acutely divisive figures: the former because of his support for Irish Republicanism and other causes regarded as extreme and the latter for his outspoken stance on immigration.

The mid-1960s to the late 1980s was a period of structural change for London. The process of deindustrialisation impacted acutely on the manufacturing and working-class areas of the city: Tower Hamlets, Hackney, Haringey, Tottenham, Kilburn, West Ham and elsewhere. Industrial unrest was only one symptom of the marked deterioration of Britain's world trading position so much so that Harold Wilson's government was forced, in 1967, to devalue the pound against the US dollar by some fourteen per cent. Decolonisation had also had the dramatic effect of increasing the flow of New Commonwealth immigrants into Britain and especially into London. Further, the oil shocks of 1973, because of the actions of OPEC, produced the debilitating conditions of 'stagflation' and London Labour Councils sought to protect local services by raising the rates. At the same time, the Labour Party's National Executive Committee abolished the list of proscribed organisations which had the effect of encouraging the tactic of 'entryism' creating a new hard core of leftist activists into urban Labour parties and especially in London. These processes began to uncouple traditional working-class support for the Labour Party in London. The new urban left had little in common with the older London working classes which was a phenomenon that Conservatives increasingly began to apprehend. Cutler's recognition that house purchase was the ambition of many 'affluent' working-class families had increasing resonance with the Conservative national leadership, especially after Margaret Thatcher had succeeded Ted Heath as Conservative leader in February 1975. The process of deindustrialisation went hand in hand with a shift to a more service-oriented economy climaxing in October 1986 with the deregulation of the stock exchange, the 'Big Bang'. Affluent workers migrated outwards to Watford, Hatfield and Welwyn and to new towns such as Stevenage, Harlow and Basildon. London boroughs, formerly occupied by poorer social groups, were also transformed and gentrified by younger professionals who sought the cachet of London living. Camden, Islington, Notting Hill and Wandsworth were all redefined as socially desirable places to live. These demographic shifts also transformed the nature of London's politics in both style and substance suggesting a newer form of the modernisation paradigm.

Thatcher's succession and her election victory in 1979 witnessed a gradual convergence of national and local issues particularly in respect of housing, and local government finance was writ large in London.[3] The ideological stance of Margaret Thatcher in this area of policy was clear enough: 'The state in the form of local authorities had frequently proved an insensitive, incompetent and corrupt landlord [and] the traditional post-war role of government in housing – that is building, ownership, management and regulation – the state should be withdrawn from these areas just as far and fast as possible'.[4] Her thinking, in respect of corruption, had been informed by research conducted by Charles Goodson-Wickes for the Centre of Policy Studies. Goodson-Wickes was trenchant in his criticism of what he regarded as the hard left who he claimed had progressively eroded the conventions of conduct in local government. Hard left councils had subverted standing orders in order to stifle opposition, and he cited Lambeth, Brent and Lewisham. Secondly, local government officers had become increasingly politicised to favour the ruling group, and he criticised Labour Councils who advertised jobs in the *Labour Weekly* and the *Morning Star*. This politicisation of officialdom was also re-enforced by the practice of cross-employment whereby councillors elected in one authority were also employed as officials in another. This raised questions of ratepayer subsidy and also the independence of the advice provided by an official who could be an official in one authority but who was also a councillor elsewhere. He also regaled those councils who used ratepayers' money to fund information campaigns and voluntary groups on the grounds that such expenditure was *ultra vires*.[5]

Dame Shirley Porter entered the maelstrom of London politics in 1974. She was the daughter of Jack Cohen who had built up the Tesco supermarket chain, and she was married to Sir Leslie Porter, the Chief Executive of the company. She was well brought up, educated privately and was a woman of immense wealth. According to her nemesis, Ken Livingstone, she was 'brassy', 'pushy' and a 'bit dim'.[6] Whether this last element of the description is fair is open to question, but she was certainly a woman driven but often lacking in political judgement. She was no match for Livingstone who was a smart operator, ruthless and an able tactician. She became Leader of Westminster City Council in 1983. Like Livingstone, she was a self-publicist who energised local politics with schemes and eye-catching task forces – 'Summer Blitzes', 'Brighter Buildings' and 'Pothole Eater Squads'. In 1986, the Conservatives had narrowly retained control of Westminster Council. Labour's leader had secured the assistance of Livingstone, now out of a job because of the abolition of the GLC, and Labour targeted three vulnerable Tory wards in Westminster: St. James, Victoria and Cavendish. In the event, the Conservatives hung on, but the narrow victories alarmed Porter and prompted her to pursue the policy of what she would call 'Building Stable Communities'. In effect, this would entail selling off council dwellings through the 'right-to-buy' scheme and gentrifying the vulnerable wards with, she hoped, Conservative voters.

The Westminster case exhibited the convergence of national policy within a special local setting. It was unusual though for corruption to be so obviously manifest in a Conservative-run local authority. It was normally a problem in Labour-controlled boroughs, which had a chequered history that stretched back to the 1930s. They were often perceived as 'fiefdoms compromised by trade union power, nepotism and the petty purchase of influence'.[7] Stepney was certainly the most notorious example although Bermondsey and Southwark were also tainted. Bermondsey was a classic Labour fiefdom in the 1930s, and according to Communist activists, Labour Bermondsey was a closed shop where business was conducted with such speed there was little opportunity to dissent. In Southwark, the Labour Party was controlled by an 'almost dynastic group, the "four families", who held power tightly in their hands, froze out newcomers and indeed discouraged membership'.[8] The politics of the LCC had often been regarded as clean, and Lord Snell claimed in 1936 that the 'breath of scandal has never touched [the Council]: its honour is very dear to all of us and to the citizens of London'. Nevertheless, the LCC elections of 1934 when Labour secured sixty-nine seats were a triumph tarnished by the claims of opponents who asserted that it was the consequence of Poplarism and the generous scales of poor relief.[9] Effectively, critics claimed, votes had been bought although this kind of rhetoric was standard fare in the aftermath of electoral defeat. The case of Stepney in the 1930s and 1940s exhibited the most flagrant example of corruption which was personified by Morry Davis, a leading Jewish politician in London's East End Politics. Davis was a founding member of the Whitechapel Labour Party and had first been elected to Stepney Council in 1924. From 1925, he had represented St. Georges and Whitechapel on the LCC. He became the Mayor of Stepney in 1930 and was elected Leader of the Council in 1935. He was immersed in Jewish communal activity and the patron of numerous organisations and charity groups. From 1935, he began to exert considerable power in controlling appointments and contracts. Labour politics in East London was riven with conflict. The area around Limehouse had been known at the time of Charles Booth's study as the Fenian Barracks. Dock labour was dominated by men of Irish descent, and it was also highly unionised, whereas Jewish immigrants were based in textiles, craft production such as furniture and various forms of self-employment.[10] Trade unions that represented municipal workers could also exert a malign influence, and in 1937 Herbert Morrison and the LCC intervened in Stepney to stop placement on unemployment relief schemes by patronage. Nevertheless, Davis was able to cultivate good working relations with Arthur Sullivan and Jerry Long, both Irish union men. Between them, they were able to dominate the Council, and Jerry Long became Mayor in 1938. Davis and Long divided the spoils influencing appointments to committees as well as the awarding of council contracts. It was Davis' high-handedness that led to a London Labour Party investigation in 1937 which discovered 'undesirable and irregular practices'.[11] Davis then purged his opponents, principally Harry Vogler who challenged Davis' use of nepotism. When London prepared for war from 1937 onwards, Davis subverted the provisions of the Air Raids Precautions Act (1937) when he secured, for himself, the position of ARP Controller, normally an appointment taken by the Town Clerk. His fondness of rewards for securing appointments was by now well known, and when Herbert Morrison was brought into Churchill's wartime cabinet as Minister for Home Security, one of his first steps was to dismiss Davis from his post as ARP Controller. Morrison's experience with Stepney and Davis no doubt influenced him when preparing the Appendix for his councillor's manual, *How London Is Governed* (1949). He was very specific on the matter of public appointments stating, 'it is contrary to good policy for members of the Council to intervene to secure appointments of individuals. Should any members disregard this rule, they would imperil the good name of the Labour Party'.[12] Morrison might have added that it was a good idea for public figures not to attempt to bribe railway ticket inspectors since Davis had tried this tactic when he had not bought a ticket. He went to gaol in 1944 for the offence.[13]

Labour councils were never far from controversy especially in the years after the Second World War. Housing shortages and LCC housing officers were not averse to taking bribes to secure flats or houses for desperate tenants. The case of such a housing officer supervising flats in Stamford Hill, Stoke Newington, resulted in a prison sentence. The Recorder, Sir Gerald Dodgson, passing sentence, stated: 'I want it to be understood that corruption is sapping the life out of the community. If it goes on national life will disintegrate as surely as that of other empires ... for no community can exist when the heart of it is eaten out by corruption'.[14] No doubt Sir Gerald was aware of the forthcoming Tribunal of Inquiry to examine the corruption of Board of Trade Minister, John Belcher.[15] Public housing and urban redevelopment schemes were obvious centres for attention particularly in the 1960s. So, in Wandsworth, the District Auditor in 1968 found that there had been overspending of £447,000 in the building department. On investigation, it was discovered that a council official had received payments from Site Caterers Ltd in 1967 for a major building project in Peckham. The official in question had shown favour to Site Caterers in return for payment and had then falsified accounts by writing off debts.[16] Wandsworth was in the headlines again in 1968. Still Labour controlled, it was one of the most damaging cases for Labour's reputation that came to light early in 1970. Investigations into the activities of Sidney Sporle, a well-respected Labour alderman, who had been Chairman of the Housing Committee before 1968, were initiated in January 1970 by the then Town Clerk Barry Payton. Wandsworth had employed the services of T. Dan Smith, the Newcastle Labour politician and self-declared expert on redevelopment. The case had also involved Interpol which had tracked down Joseph Capo-Bianco, a consultant engineer, who, like Smith, had been employed on a consultancy basis. Capo-Bianco was arrested and charged under the Corruption of Public Bodies Act 1889. The case revolved around a £6.5 million housing development for Wandsworth, and it emerged that Sporle had accepted a £500 inducement to offer the contract to John Laing Construction. Additionally, he had accepted payments from Smith to show favour to one of Smith's consultancy companies, Fleet Press Services Limited. Smith had first promoted himself with Wandsworth in January 1966 when he expounded on the virtues of public relations in major building and redevelopment projects. Sporle was present at this meeting and later accepted retainer payments from Fleet Press Services. At crucial meetings of the Housing Committee and the full council, Sporle failed to declare his interests. Sporle and his wife, who was also a councillor in Wandsworth, were also found to have accepted hospitality from Laing's, including theatre trips to London's West End. Capo-Bianco, too, had accepted hospitality both in England and abroad. Sporle, Capo-Bianco and Peter Day, another construction engineer, were found guilty. Smith, however, was acquitted and the police reported that he had not attempted to conceal his payments to Sporle.[17] This presupposed that the fees had not been made corruptly. Rather, it was Sporle's failure to declare an interest that was the easier to pursue. The fact that the Wandsworth case was part of a network of corrupt activity that had been promoted by T. Dan Smith and John Poulson may have caused the opprobrium normally attendant in such cases to become dispersed more generally.

Nevertheless, Labour's reputation in local government, generally, and in London in particular was not assisted by the Wandsworth case.

Lambeth and Hackney, both Labour controlled in the early 1980s, had been heavily criticised by their respective auditors. Lambeth, led by the leftist Ted Knight had been challenged in the courts for raising the rates whilst freezing council rents, and the spokesman for the group that invoked the court action claimed that Lambeth had 'the reputation of being the most profligate local authority in Britain'.[18] Later Geoffrey Finsberg, Under Secretary of State for the Environment, accused Lambeth of driving business away and pushing up unemployment: 'They have chosen a cheap and cowardly way for making others pay for their own pet political theories'.[19] Knight and his supporters were defiant, setting a supplementary rate to bridge the gap created by the cut in the rate support grant. Knight taunted the government by dubbing the additional levy as the 'Heseltine Rate'.[20] The conflict rumbled on throughout the early 1980s, and when the Council refused to set a new rate for 1985–86, the District Auditor, Brian Skinner, informed thirty-one Lambeth councillors, including Knight, that they would be surcharged on the grounds that the Council had been faced with a 'loss ... caused by the wilful misconduct of the councillors'.[21] Lambeth was not alone in this respect. Councillors in Camden and Islington were also faced with surcharge. In Hackney, the District Auditor found that £3.7million of grants disbursed earlier in 1983–84 to a range of community groups were mismanaged and that there were 'serious deficiencies in financial control'.[22] These cases suggested mismanagement and inefficiency rather than corruption, but left-wing councils were still able to obstruct the government for long periods in what has often been portrayed as an ideological struggle between a *dirigiste* central government and the champions of local democracy. However, this obscured the fact that there had been a long history of malpractice and corruption in Lambeth that dated back to 1968–71 when it was Conservative controlled and John Major was a Lambeth councillor. Additionally, in 1977, the Council had been forced to admit that 1.7 million bricks, sufficient to build 2,000 houses, had been lost. A Council spokesman was reduced to the feeble excuse that there had been a lack of precision in the recording of receipts. In 1970, the Council had been forced to conduct an inquiry when a housebuilding project estimated at £500,000 ran at thirty per cent over budget. Further, in 1987 the Council Leader, Linda Bellos, set up an independent inquiry into Lambeth's construction services, and the subsequent report revealed inefficiency and alleged corruption in the direct labour scheme over a number of years. There were also indications that Ted Knight continued to have links with a firm, Building Contractors Ltd, of which he had been a former director, and that the firm had secured Council contracts worth £400,000. Finally, an internal investigation headed by Herman Ouseley itemised maladministration, fraud and inefficiency that had cost the Council £10 million. It was, he said, an 'abysmal legacy'.[23] Thus, when Lambeth advertised for a new chief executive, eventually securing Heather Rabbatts from Merton, she inherited a council that had £200 million in debts that was also the subject of no fewer than twenty-five different inquiries. According to one councillor, 'If Hercules himself had been made chief executive, he'd have given up and gone away', and another remarked that it was like trying to 'tame Dodge City'.[24] However, the Council had commissioned a further investigation to be conducted by Elizabeth Appleby QC. She was an extremely experienced lawyer, as well as being Chairman of the Conservative Party's Ethics and Integrity Committee. She found that 500 out of 10,000 staff were involved in housing benefit fraud and that there was a deliberate council policy 'to protect its own workforce at all costs'. There had also been numerous instances of poor financial control. For example, a building scheme for 150 homes had skyrocketed from £4.2 million to £8.1 million, and she agreed with the District Auditor that overspending on highway maintenance was illegal because the Council had not followed proper tendering regulations. Heather Rabbatts welcomed the report even though it revealed a 'catastrophic litany' of 'waste and corruption'.[25] The claim of Ted Knight that he and his fellow councillors had fought to save the Borough from Tory underfunding was seemingly exploded. 'I plead guilty to fighting the Thatcher government [and] we had to protect services for the people'.[26] He claimed that Labour's national leadership failed to mount a serious campaign against the Tories and this had in turn produced a conflict inside the Party between the leadership and the activists resulting in a failure to connect with 'the broader public'.[27] He had failed on both fronts. Appleby's Report repudiated the argument that Lambeth's problems had emanated from underfunding. It was the result, she said, of years of 'political feuding, mismanagement and incompetence by the Labour regime'.[28] She also pointed out that it had been necessary to dismiss thirty employees because it was clear that 'recruitment in the borough bore the signs of nepotism'.[29] Labour's national leadership could see that there was no way out of the stranglehold that Appleby's Report exerted. Frank Dobson candidly admitted that Labour's performance from 1979 to 1993 had been disgraceful. He also disowned Lambeth's irresponsible leadership. Kate Hoey, the Labour MP for Vauxhall, was equally realistic in her comment on Labour's poor showing in the council by election in Lambeth in 1993, when she said that the voters had had enough of 'corruption, rotten administration and inefficiency'.[30] The Lambeth case was perhaps an extreme example where ideological intransigence on the part of central government and the leftist faction led by Knight combined with other problems: patronage in employment, trade union defence of the Council's direct labour organisation, inadequate financial control, fraud and underqualified staff.

The history of Labour's conduct in London politics then was a mixture of technocratic idealism as expounded by Sidney Webb and Harold Laski and which ostensibly pervaded the workings of the LCC until it was replaced by the GLC and machine politics in the London boroughs where class, ethnicity and religion generated loyalties and allegiances that were more powerful than the canons of ethical conduct and probity that had been inherited from the nineteenth century. In the Labour boroughs, there was a hard-headed politics that commanded discipline, loyalty and reward not dissimilar to American 'pork barrel' politics[31] and modes of conduct that could often result in corruption.

By contrast, Westminster was an efficient and well-run council. It had been lauded, along with Wandsworth, now regarded as a flagship council controlled by Conservatives since 1978. Moreover, Lady Porter's publicity-seeking style had seemed to fit with the prestigious associations of the City of Westminster – the Houses of Parliament, Downing Street and Trafalgar Square. Thus, after a short period of intense consultation with officers, independent consultants and legal advice from Jeremy Sullivan QC, later a high court judge, Porter presented a paper in 1988 to the Westminster Conservatives called 'Keeping Westminster Conservative': 'Imagine socialists running Buckingham Palace, militants lording it over Parliament and controlling Downing Street, left-wing extremists interfering in the daily running of business, a horrible nightmare'.[32] The scale of the subsequent operation involved a range of the Council's departments including planning, public relations and of course housing. The Porter gerrymandering case developed following the local government elections of 1986 when the Conservatives under Porter's leadership lost eleven seats. The council chamber was now much more finely balanced with the Conservatives with thirty-two and Labour with twenty-seven representatives. Under Porter's initiative, the Conservatives identified eight key wards: Cavendish, Victoria, St. James, Millbank, West End, Bayswater, Little Venice and Hamilton Terrace. Using the government's 'right-to-buy' legislation, Westminster Council sought to gentrify the eight key wards by means of a programme of the sale of council homes to new owners who it was thought would vote Conservative.[33] Specifically, this would involve the creation of 2,200 new voters across the key wards. In this sense then, the Westminster scandal was not technically gerrymandering as it did not and could not involve the redrawing of ward boundaries to alter the composition of the electorate to favour the ruling party. Boundaries were determined independently by the Local Government Boundary Commission for England.[34] In fact, it was a plan to engineer the social demography within the eight key wards in the belief that new homeowners would vote Conservative. It also entailed moving out what were perceived to be potential Labour voters, and it had also involved irregularities in the compilation of the electoral register since, apparently, students, nurses and people living in hostel accommodation had been misinformed by the Council as to their voting rights.[35] In electoral terms, the policy was a success as Porter and the Conservatives secured a thumping victory in the local elections of May 1990. They won forty-five out of sixty seats and Labour was reduced to fifteen seats. The implications of the case were far reaching, and Labour activists were even hopeful that it would bring down John Major's government.

The demographic and structural changes that London had experienced from the mid-1960s to 1987 were immense. Those changes had altered the character of the London Labour parties especially in the gentrified boroughs – Camden and Islington – and Labour activists had become increasingly middle class, educated and overtly ideological in temper and libertarian in attitude. Labour's politics became the politics of posture and advocacy often focused on what were regarded as fringe issues. This was coupled with the fact that it was Labour-controlled boroughs that had previously been tainted with charges of misconduct, corruption, inefficiency as well as the causes of the 'loony left'. The popular press had frequently drawn attention to the GLC's publicity campaigns for left-wing pressure group causes – 'Gay London Police Monitoring Group' and 'Babies against the Bomb' to name but two. Indeed, Margaret Thatcher had commissioned a special report for the Conservatives which argued that numerous London Boroughs – all Labour controlled – had spending programmes in breach of Section 137 of the Local Government Act 1972. For example, the Borough of Brent's claims that it was a 'nuclear-free zone', Camden's 'Peace Group Steering Committee' and Islington's funding of a local newspaper, *The Islington Gazette*, were all cast as *ultra vires* by a Centre for Policy Studies paper, *The New Corruption*.[36] But perhaps most controversial was the GLC campaign in support of the IRA. These instances were not cases of corruption perhaps in any conventional legal sense although they were probably cases of misconduct. Thus, the Westminster case provided Labour with an opportunity to turn the tables. The issue represented a classic polarisation of views, and for once Labour was able to adopt the moral high ground: Andrew Dismore, the Labour Leader on the Westminster Council, excoriated the Conservatives saying that it revealed a 'shameful and illegal management of the Council by the Tories for party political electoral advantage'.[37] Thus, for Labour's national leadership, it was an opportunity to be seized upon. Jack Straw, then Labour's Shadow Environment Secretary, openly talked of seeking financial support from trade unions to assist those Westminster community charge payers who had taken legal action against Westminster. Contemporaries regarded this as indicative of the Labour leadership's view of 'how useful it believes the Westminster gerrymandering allegations will prove', and perhaps they hoped that it would deflect attention from 'accusations of inefficiency and corruption regularly levelled against Labour run councils'.[38] Perhaps one of the most notable instances of such claims was made by the Conservative Party Chairman, Jeremy Hanley, in the run-up to the local elections of May 1995: 'Throughout the country there are examples of mismanagement, of councils with high taxes, profligate spending, incompetence, waste and corruption. There are very many examples of corruption in Labour councils, but particularly poor services and political posturing'.[39] This was no doubt a reference to Ted Knight and the Lambeth councillors who had refused to set a rate but still found time to go on an expenses paid fact-finding mission to Nicaragua in

1985. Hanley also singled out Haringey. Frank Dobson, Labour's front-bench spokesman, retorted that Hanley was 'beneath contempt' and 'not up to the job'. John Major, too, in a prime ministerial answer to a question from David Shaw, MP for Dover, held the Tory line although he was more circumspect when he said, 'I have no doubt that there are many cases of waste and inefficiency and malpractice in Labour councils and increasingly one has seen that in auditors' reports'.[40]

The Conservatives by contrast were relatively clean. The Westminster case of the late 1980s where the Leader of the Council, Dame Shirley Porter, was able to suborn officials and councillors must be explained. The status of local government as a partner of central government had been reinforced by the war years and the reforms of Attlee's post-war government which had made local government a principal agent of national government's aim to build a New Jerusalem. In many respects, although there is an emerging revisionist school of interpretation, local government was part of the post-war consensus since it was charged with delivering the principal cornerstones of the new society – education, health and housing.[41] However, the appearance of consensus is somewhat misleading, and although the Macmillan government fought toe to toe with Labour to build municipal dwellings, there was always a deep-rooted commitment in the Conservative Party to a property owning democracy. Anthony Eden at the Conservative Party Conference had delivered a clarion call for a 'nationwide property owning democracy'. This was not just idealism but rather a political calculation that the relationship between municipal landlords and council house tenants created an allegiance and dependence to Labour in both national and local elections. In 1953, Macmillan appointed Ernest Marples to investigate alternatives to public housing controlled by local authorities. This would entail entertaining different forms of co-ownership. The Treasury, however, was sceptical and initiatives to engage building societies and insurance companies failed. Attempts to promote the private rental market with the Rent Act 1957 were also unsuccessful. The idea of co-ownership continued to buzz in a few Tory ears, principally those of Henry Brooke, who had experience on the LCC. Additionally, 'The One Nation Group' which included Keith Joseph, Iain MacLeod and Enoch Powell was also attracted to the idea of co-ownership, and Henry Brooke secured support from Dame Evelyn Sharp, the Permanent Secretary. The Treasury's objections hinged around the problem that co-ownership was in fact a concealed subsidy. Nevertheless, the Housing Act 1961 created a £25 million fund from which loans on generous terms for housing associations and trusts to arrange co-ownership schemes. The programme was not a panacea and some 40,000 homes were built under the co-ownership legislation between 1964 and 1966. This new form of tenure provided the Conservatives with an alternative model to local authority housing that involved, according to Lord Woolton, 'herding of more people into these huge County Council housing areas, which become predominantly socialist in political outlook'.[42] Essentially, the experiment in co-ownership was born of political weakness when Labour had won the political argument to promote local authority housing. Nevertheless, the idea was gaining traction within the Tories. The outspoken Horace Cutler, for example, suggested, in a television interview in 1969, that 'local authorities ought to get out of housing ... because they don't know how to run it'.[43] Crucially, he recognised the aspirations of what he called 'two car tenants' who wanted to own their own homes. Cutler's views were to gain ground after 1978.

The Conservative commitment to the principle of homeownership had a long pedigree as the statements of Eden, Woolton and Brooke revealed. In 1978, Michael Heseltine restated the Conservative position in a Conservative Research Department paper. He recognised that the rate of council house-building had been greater than the rate of sales to tenants. Between 1970 and 1977, local authorities had sold off 130,000 council houses. However, the number of council house-building starts over the same period exceeded 990,000. Heseltine's case for sales argued that council house sales would spread wealth along with wider ownership, but like his predecessors, he believed that it would promote 'independence from the state'. There was also an important economic argument: simply, the costs of building and the Exchequer subsidy far exceeded the income derived by local authorities from rent. Additionally, tenants in older houses had in some cases paid more in rent than the cost of the house to the local authority. This would appeal to voters who aspired to own their own homes since it was argued that rent payments were subsidising the building of new houses and that the tenant had paid a lifetime's rent with no 'asset at the end'. Heseltine put forward a scheme to make the sale of council houses much easier with more realistic valuations, with discounts for sitting tenants ranging between thirty and fifty per cent, with more generous mortgages and an arrangement with the legal profession to charge a flat rate fee for conveyancing and contracts. Finally, for a party intent on reducing the size of the state and lowering the Public Sector Borrowing Requirement, the capital receipts from the sales represented a most attractive proposition.[44]

It has often been claimed that the Conservatives liked local government because it provided a challenge to the burgeoning socialist state. When Margaret Thatcher became MP for Finchley, she sought to make a name for herself and quickly promoted a private member's bill – Public Bodies (Admission of the Press to Meetings) Bill in November 1959. Thatcher had discussed the framing and drafting of the Bill with Evelyn Sharp, and it seemed that the new MP's proposals struck a chord as the Department 'had it in mind to agree a "code of behaviour" with the representatives of local authorities'.[45] Thatcher was no doubt prescient with the claim in her maiden speech when she claimed, 'Publicity is the greatest and most effective check against arbitrary action'.[46] The convergence of the idea of a code of behaviour and open meetings with access for the press was almost a first clause in an anti-corruption charter.

Appearances were deceptive, and as often was the case with Thatcher's politics, it was also partisan as she regarded Labour-controlled authorities as the culprits of secrecy and *in camera* meetings.[47] Thus, there were two clear themes emerging. Firstly, the Conservatives sought an opportunity to promote an alternative to public housing controlled by local authorities, and secondly Thatcher was disposed to break the Labour fiefdoms. Indeed, she saw local government as one of the three repositories of 'hard left' power. The other two were the Labour Party itself and the trade unions.[48] After 1979, this was to become a centre piece in her policies. Further, the case of gerrymandering in Westminster, although an unintended consequence of national government policy, was symptomatic of these two themes: the promotion of homeownership to break Labour's patronage of council tenants and that in a favoured flagship council such as Westminster then Conservative electoral advantage had to be maintained, as Shirley Porter saw it, at all costs. Porter was prone to present herself as Thatcher's counterpart in local government determined to break Labour in its traditional bastions.[49]

Following the local elections of May 1990 which had been a Conservative triumph in Westminster, twelve Westminster residents submitted objections to the District Auditor. Their claim that the designated sales programme in particular wards was unlawful should not have been a surprise to Porter and her supporters since at the inception of the plan, the Westminster Council's solicitor, Matthew Ives, had warned of the danger that the scheme might have the appearance of a political 'machination'. According to Paul Dimoldenberg, Labour Leader at the time, the Council's deputy solicitor, Robert Lewis, consulted Jeremy Sullivan QC in May 1987 who advised that selling homes in the eight key wards alone was illegal and that any sales must be for legitimate reasons and apply to all wards across the City of Westminster. Remarkably, Lewis chose not to share this information.[50] According to Andrew Hosken, the BBC journalist who investigated the case, the truth was more complicated. According to Hosken, Graham England, the Director of Housing, Paul Hayler, a senior housing officer, and Lewis met with Sullivan at his Gray's Inn chambers. Sullivan's advice was clear that targeting the marginal wards alone was unlawful. However, England and Hayler claimed that the Council's own consultants, PA Cambridge, had outlined 'justifications'. Sullivan apparently qualified his view saying that preventing polarisation of owner-occupiers and tenants and enabling skilled workers to remain in Westminster were all potential justifications. These qualifications were sufficient to convince the officers that they could tell Porter what she wanted to hear.[51] In fact, it became *carte blanche* to expand the designated sales programme. However, no matter how the interpretation of the law might be nuanced, the District Auditor's Report revealed the recklessness of the scheme which cost the Council £21.25 million. Of particular importance in understanding the ruthlessness with which 'Building Stable Communities' was pursued, John Magill's breakdown was especially revealing: the Council sold off local authority dwellings with such large discounts that the Council incurred £13.3 million in costs, the boarding up and securing empty homes together with loss of rent amounted to £1.6 million and the costs of temporary accommodation, often outside the Borough's boundaries, amounted to £2 million.[52] In fact, the operation of the designated sales programme involved closing down hotels and bed and breakfast accommodation and with the Council purchasing them for residential use to be converted to flats for sale. The plans to sell the Ambrosden Hostel to private developers prompted the intervention of Cardinal Basil Hume who asked that Westminster reconsider.[53] The people displaced were rehoused in other parts of London such as Tooting and Streatham. The Westminster City Architect's Department even drew up plans to build temporary accommodation of prefabricated design located in Barking. By 1988, the Council had identified over 2,400 properties that could be sold directly or could be disposed by means of assisted purchase. The largest concentrations were in Bayswater and Millbank where 1,400 properties fell into the plan. In Little Venice, it was planned to sell off over 400 properties. The remainder, ranging between 100 and 150 homes per ward, were in Cavendish, Hamilton Terrace, St. James and Victoria.[54] The Environment Secretary was shocked by the 'unambiguous findings of the Report'.[55] Dame Shirley Porter refuted Magill's claims, claiming that her own legal advice stated that Magill's findings were incorrect and unfair. John Major displayed his usual caution because of the provisional nature of the Report. In addition to Dame Shirley, a number of other councillors and officers were identified as potentially liable for surcharge. They were David Weeks, Deputy Leader, and Porter's general factotum. He had, apparently, contempt for officers.[56] Graham England had been Director of Housing since September 1985. Bill Phillips was an experienced civil servant who had been seconded from the Department of the Environment to advise on the Building Stable Communities project. Barry Legg was the Conservative Chief Whip and was to become the MP for Milton Keynes South-West. Judith Warner had been joint Chairman of the Housing Committee along with Dr Michael Dutt who was an ambitious career politician who had stood unsuccessfully as an MEP in 1989 and also as an MP for Leicester South in 1992. He became joint Chairman of the Housing Committee with Warner in February 1988. He was an enthusiast for Building Stable Communities and 'would exert a malign influence on the communities of Westminster'.[57] Within a fortnight of the publication of Magill's Report, he committed suicide.

After the publication of Magill's Report, Westminster Council mounted a post hoc rationalisation and defence. It merits some examination. Graham England expressed the view that council members were, after the 1986 elections, surprised by the low level of voter registration. According to England, drawing on the PA Cambridge Report, this was because many residents in Westminster were employed by offshore companies particularly banks and finance companies which bought accommodation to rent to their employees whilst they were based in London. These people may or may not have worked in the borough, but they did not register to vote. At the same time, in the 'seedier parts of north Westminster private landlords had begun to let homes for prostitutes or holidaymakers'.[58] According to England, the Council resolved to tighten planning controls and use its stock of municipal housing under the government's right to buy scheme: 'You can't take on Japanese banks on the open market but you can persuade middle income families into Westminster'.[59] He went on to claim that Jack Straw and others had misrepresented the Council's policy and that the Council had not deliberately sold houses to yuppies. He also denied the claims of social cleansing to force the homeless out of the Borough. Somewhat disingenuously, he claimed that the policy – moving people out – created jealousy amongst Westminster residents:

> I've been offered the Mozart estate [Kilburn]. Why are you giving this place to a Bosnian refugee, I'd like a house with a garden in Hillingdon.[60]

The Westminster corruption case is perhaps one of the most difficult to assess. It was not obviously gerrymandering as had been practised in American politics or indeed in Irish politics where the Unionists brazenly redrew ward boundaries in Londonderry to the advantage of their own party. Porter and her associates sought legal advice on how to use existing legislation for the sale of council dwellings. It has also been suggested that the District Auditor, John Magill, was inexperienced and unfamiliar with local government but more crucially pursued a personal vendetta against Porter for his own ends, specifically to increase his fees.[61] He had seized some 6,000 council documents as part of an investigation which had consumed his life since July 1989, and he did not report until March 1994. He had conducted 133 interviews with fifty individuals. Perhaps Magill's approach was obsessive, but the Local Government Finance Act (1982) required the District Auditor to 'recover losses incurred or deficiency caused by the wilful misconduct of any person ... and the loss or deficiency is due from that person'.[62] At the same time, it should not be forgotten that Labour, too, had resorted to questionable tactics. Labour activists had promoted squatters occupations in properties designated for sale and had disrupted council and committee meetings where the police had to be called to secure the safety of councillors. Further, Ken Livingstone's use of £32,000 of GLC funds to promote the Westminster Registration Project to encourage ethnic minorities to register in the belief that they would vote Labour was an example of the use of public money for party political advantage. In 1984, Livingstone had also authorised £8,000 to support a Westminster tenants group that was protesting against the council's housing policies.[63] Nevertheless, Lord Bingham found against Porter and her deputy David Weeks ruling that the intention of Building Stable Communities was gerrymandering and that adjustment in the designated sales policy was just a 'smokescreen' to 'disguise gerrymandering in the marginal [wards]'.

The legal battle persisted through to May 2003, but crucially in 2001, the House of Lords upheld Magill. Lord Bingham summarised saying that Porter and Weeks had perpetrated a 'blatant and dishonest use of public power'. Lord Scott was equally clear saying that the case was one of 'political corruption. The corruption was not money corruption. No one took a bribe. There are other forms of corruption, often less easily detectable and therefore more insidious ... Gerrymandering engenders cynicism about elections, about politicians and their motives and damages the reputation of democratic government'.[64] Finally, her claim that she was treated unfairly was thrown out by the European Court of Human Rights in May 2003. Dame Shirley Porter then proved just as divisive a figure as Livingstone and Cutler.

Her supporters point to her charitable endeavours, not just in Israel but also in Britain with support for the Royal Academy and the National Portrait Gallery. Additionally, Conservative activists such as Phillip Jones, the Chairman of the Mid-Staffordshire Conservative Association, wrote to *The Times* pleading that she 'did not enrich herself'.[65] She had no need to do so. William Rees-Mogg claimed that Magill made an error of judgement in holding a press conference to announce his findings before he had released his Report, and should have resigned; and, moreover, that he was 'insensitive and may not have been capable of judging his own degree of bias'.[66] Her opponents regard her as abrasive, arrogant, hectoring and self-seeking. Both Conservatives and Labour in London in the late 1980s resorted to extreme measures to capture the headlines, and Building Stable Communities was just one such example. Since the Porter case, the Nolan Commission has observed that the instrument of surcharging councillors is an unsatisfactory device and the Labour Government in fact legislated against surcharging in the Local Government Act 2000. That may be so but it remains the case that the 'homes for votes' scandal in Westminster as presented in the Auditor's Report was a 'devastating account of the wholesale subversion of a council's operations to further the interests of the ruling party'.[67] Moreover, politics had fallen into a 'pit of dishonour'[68] where council officers had been cowed into timidity and fear so much so that, according to the Auditor, the 'permeability between party politics and council business corrupted the democratic process'.[69]

After Porter's final failure to avoid surcharge, she pleaded poverty although she was living in luxury accommodation in Israel and holidaying in Palm Springs. She also claimed that she was the victim of a 'vendetta with overtones of jealousy and anti-Semitism'.[70] Nevertheless, Westminster City Council succeeded in freezing her assets and required courts around the world to disclose the value of her wealth. Orders were granted in England, Guernsey and the British Virgin Islands.[71] In August 2010, the Communities' Secretary, Eric Pickles, announced that the Audit Commission would be scrapped claiming, 'The corporate centre of the Audit Commission has lost its way. Rather than being a watchdog that champions taxpayers' interests, it has become the creature of the Whitehall state ... We need to redress this balance. Audit should remain to ensure taxpayers' money is properly spent, but this can be done in a competitive environment, drawing on professional audit expertise across the country'.[72] Although the Nolan Commission had been critical of the practice of surcharging and therefore presumably welcomed its abolition in 2000, it expressed dismay that almost half of all local authorities had not adopted the new standards regime and moreover that new arrangements proposed by the government rested on 'relatively modest sanctions' and a reduction in 'independent scrutiny'.[73] John Magill had provided such independent scrutiny. He may have been a zealot, but after a battle lasting almost ten years, his position was upheld.

Notes

1 Machiavelli, *The Discourses* (1970), p. 118.
2 John Magill, *Final Audit Report for Westminster City Council*, Audit Commission (May 1996).
3 Weiler, P., 'The conservatives' search for a middle-way in housing, 1951–64', *Twentieth Century British History*, 14: 4 (2003), pp. 360–90.
4 Margaret Thatcher, *Downing Street Years* (London: Harper Collins, 1993), pp. 599–600.
5 Goodson-Wickes, C., *The New Corruption* (London: Centre for Policy Studies, 1984), pp. 19–25.
6 Livingstone, K., *You Can't Say That: Memoirs* (London: Faber and Faber, 2011), p. 268.
7 White, J., *London in the Twentieth Century: A City and Its People* (London: Vintage, 2008), p. 377.
8 Goss, S., *Local Labour and Local Government: A Study in Changing Interests, Politics and Policy in Southwark from 1919 to 1982* (Edinburgh: Edinburgh University Press, 1988), p. 45, 55.
9 Poplar Council had led a vigorous campaign for the equalisation of poor rates across London. In 1921, thirty-six Labour councillors had been served writs for failure to set a rate. See also Marriott, J., *Beyond the Tower: A History of East London* (New Haven and London: Yale University Press, 2011), pp. 278–9.
10 Marriott, *Beyond the Tower*.
11 White, *London*, p. 378; Alderman, G., *London Jewry and London Politics, 1889–1986* (London: Christopher Helm, 1989); and Smith, E.R., *East End Jews: Politics 1918–1939: A Study in Class and Ethnicity* (University of Leicester, Unpublished PhD thesis, 1990).
12 Morrison, *How London Is Governed* (1949), pp. 169–70.
13 White, *London*, p. 377.
14 *The Times*, 28 October 1948.
15 *Bribery of Ministers of the Crown or Other Public Servants in Connection with the Grant of Licences* (1948), Cmd., 7616.
16 *The Times*, 17 April 1968, 12 October 1968.
17 Fitzwalter, R., *Web of Corruption: the story of J.G.L. Poulson and T. Dan Smith* (Granada, London, 1981) and *The Times*, 19 January 1970, 4 March 1970, 24 March 1971, 1 July 1971.

18 *The Times*, 20 May 1980.
19 Geoffrey Finsberg quoted in *The Times*, 13 January 1981.
20 Ted Knight, letter to *The Times*, 26 January 1981.
21 *The Times*, 11 September 1985.
22 *The Times*, 27 July 1985.
23 *The Guardian*, 22 May 1993.
24 *The Guardian*, 10 December 1994.
25 *The Guardian*, 29 July 1995.
26 *Ibid*.
27 Rodrigues, J. interview with Ted Knight in *Marxism Today* (January 1981).
28 *The Guardian*, 28 July 1995.
29 *The Guardian*, 4 August 1995.
30 *The Guardian*, 30 March 1993.
31 'Pork barrel' politics involves the allocation of public funds in the form of building projects, work schemes and welfare programmes by means of reciprocal deals between elected representatives.
32 Shirley Porter quoted in Hosken, A., *Nothing Like a Dame: The Scandals of Shirley Porter* (London: Granta, 2006), p. 225.
33 For studies of gentrification, see Hamnett, C. and P. Williams, 'Social change in London: a study of gentrification', *The London Journal*, 6 (1980), pp. 51–66.
34 *Local Government Boundary Commission for England, Report*, 413 (1981) and Report 627 (1992).
35 *Local Government Chronicle*, 4 March 1994.
36 Goodson-Wickes, *New Corruption*.
37 *Local Government Chronicle*, 18 February 1994.
38 *Local Government Chronicle*, 28 January 1994.
39 *The Guardian*, 18 March 1995.
40 HC Debates, 16 March 1995, vol. 256, cc. 1021–4.
41 See Kavanagh, D., *Thatcherism and British Politics: The End of Consensus* (Oxford: Oxford University Press, 1987) sets out the challenge to consensus argument; pp. 64–101. For an alternative interpretation Pimlott, B., 'The myth of consensus', in Smith, L. (ed.), *The Making of Britain: Echoes of Greatness* (London: Macmillan, 1988) and Vinen, R., *Thatcher's Britain: The Politics and Social Upheaval of the 1980s* (London: Pocket Books, 2010).
42 Quoted in Weiler, 'The conservatives' search', pp. 360–90.
43 John Davis, 'Cutler, Sir Horace Walter 1912–97', *Oxford Dictionary of National Biography*, www.odnb.com, visited on 6 August 2012.
44 Michael Heseltine, 'The Sale of Council Houses' Shadow Cabinet Circulated paper 28 June 1978, MTFW Thatcher MSS 2/6/1/163, www.margaretthatcher.org, visited on 27 February 2012.
45 Dame Evelyn Sharp, Minute 2 December 1959, MTFW, Private Members Bill, HLG 29/490.
46 HC Debates, vol. 616, cc. 1350–8.
47 Vincent, *The Culture of Secrecy* (1998).
48 Thatcher, *Downing Street Years*, p. 339.
49 Shirley Porter, *Minister for London: A Capital Concept* (London: FPL Financial Ltd., 1990).

50 Dimoldenberg, P., *The Westminster Whistle Blowers: Shirley Porter, Homes for Votes and Twenty Years of Scandal in Britain's Rottenest Borough* (London: Politico, 2006), pp. 19–20. Dimoldenberg's book is a passionate and invaluable account of the 'homes for votes' scandal.

51 Hosken, *Nothing Like a Dame*, pp. 146–7.

52 Magill, *Audit Report for Westminster City Council*.

53 Hosken, *Nothing Like a Dame*, p. 161.

54 Hosken, *Nothing Like a Dame*, pp. 153–6, p. 197.

55 *Local Government Chronicle*, 21 January 1994.

56 Hosken, *Nothing Like a Dame*, p. 77.

57 Hosken, *Nothing Like a Dame*, p. 217.

58 *Local Government Chronicle*, 21 January 1994.

59 Graham England quoted in *Local Government Chronicle*, 21 January 1994.

60 *Ibid*.

61 Jones, G.W., 'In defence of Dame Shirley Porter', *Local Government Studies*, 35: 1 (2009), pp. 143–52.

62 *Lloyd v. McMahon* (1987) *UKHL*, 5, 12 March 1987, www.baillii.org.uk, visited on 27 February 2012.

63 Jones, 'In defence of Dame Shirley Porter', pp. 143–52.

64 Quoted in *The Times*, 31 May 2003.

65 Letter to *The Times*, 9 December 2003.

66 Rees-Mogg, W., in *The Times*, 17 December 2001.

67 *The Observer*, 12 May 1996.

68 *The Guardian*, 12 May 1996.

69 Magill quoted in *The Guardian*, 12 May 1996.

70 *The Times*, 8 March 2004.

71 *The Times*, 5 Nov. 2003.

72 BBC News, 13 August 2010.

73 Sir Christopher Kelly, Chairman of the Committee on Standards in Public Life. *Press Release*, 28 June 2012.

Conclusion

What then are the principal causes of corruption in modern British urban society? According to political science, the causes are to be located within the frameworks prescribed by elite theory, modernisation and transition theory and the complex processes of state building. According to sociologists, corruption is a social–political construction shaped by prevailing social structure and processes such as stratification, social mobility and the conflict between sub-cultural norms and wider public values. For economists, the causes are to be found in the interaction between public bureaucratic markets and free markets. Cultural theorists maintain that the causes of corrupt behaviour reside in the nature of the prevailing ethical environment, in the degree of trust present in human transactions and in the stock of social capital available to sustain a vibrant civil society.

This study has tried to demonstrate the value of these theoretical causal factors. There is little doubt that the party fiefdoms of the north of England were elite structures underpinned by party machines. Because of regional aid patterns and a range of client networks, the political bosses were able to broker deals between national and local governments and maintain their political grip. Poulson bought into this network by providing hospitality, gifts, commissions and retainers in exchange for building contracts.

Although general theories provide valuable analytical tools of analysis, it is clear that the historically specific circumstances of the period c. 1930–95 were special. The Glasgow case revealed that the established urban patriciate was replaced by a new elite that had to 'live by politics' and so resorted to corruption. However, those that 'lived' for politics, John McGovern and Patrick Dollan, conducted their campaign against corruption in the language of the older urban patriciate that they had supplanted. They extolled the reputation of the Glasgow Corporation and lauded the virtues of probity, integrity and honesty anticipating their resurrection by Lord Nolan some sixty years later.

It should not be forgotten though that Glasgow in the 1930s was a pitiless city that exhibited many of the worst pathologies of urban life – insanitary housing, ill health, street violence, alcoholism and gambling – and perhaps corrupt dealings were just a way of getting by.

The corruptions of Poulson, Smith, Maudling, Cunningham and Sporle might seem to fit in terms of sociological theory: they rationalised their own behaviour in terms of their subcultural group. Their world was coherent and ordered in which entertainment, commissions and fees were acceptable. What is more challenging though is the relationship of their actions to urban processes, generated initially by a modernisation impulse that involved the rebuilding of the urban environment with new sources of funding, new building technologies and experts such as town planners and civil servants. Housing contracts, town centre developments, schools, colleges, new universities, and leisure facilities constituted part of the modernisation process. It brought together architects, planners, solicitors, businessmen and politicians who interacted in transactions that fostered corrupt dealings. Further, the bureaucratic hurdles – budget priorities, tendering processes, planning regulations and civil service protocols – invited often corrupt solutions. The rebuilding of urban Britain involved interaction between bureaucratic and free enterprise markets. Additionally, central government money passed through various conduits – regional aid, new town corporations as well as the rate support grant – that created numerous opportunities for the would-be corrupt. Moreover, the entertainment budgets of companies such as Laing, Bovis and Wimpey were considerable. In some senses, the conduct of those in the Poulson–Smith ring was little different to the opportunism of speculative builders in the eighteenth and nineteenth centuries or the municipal councillor of the nineteenth century who was privy to the enactment of a boundary extension and became involved in land deals. In the post-1945 era, chairing the planning committee of a local authority was an extremely powerful position, and membership of the committee was much coveted simply because its decisions could influence the value of property, especially in resorts such as Blackpool. Whether corruption revived in the 1960s and 1970s to create a corrupt moment might suggest a change in the ethical environment, but opinion polls imply a healthy suspicion of politicians and their motives. The role of the press and investigative journalism, television and radio brought the issue of corruption into living rooms throughout the land, and so new technologies and forms of media communication – the documentary and the radio phone-in, for example – created new possibilities of participation, sensitising public consciousness to the issue of corruption and lowering the public tolerance threshold in the process. Lastly, the Porter case represented something both modern but also traditional. In the 1970s and 1980s, London experienced dramatic changes – deindustrialisation, the sale of council housing, the deregulation of the stock exchange and the complex process of gentrification – and these changes created unique opportunities to secure political advantage. However, the motives of the corrupt were traditional: elite preservation.

The Nolan Commission's stance that it could teach the Seven Principles of Public Life – selflessness, integrity, objectivity, accountability, openness, honesty and leadership – sounds more like an 'awayday' for committed public sector managers. It will not appeal to recalcitrant politicians who jealously guard their privileges. In its Third Report in 1997, the Nolan Commission recommended the establishment of a new ethical framework which included a code of conduct for local councillors, not imposed but developed by each individual council; the establishment of a Standards Committee in each council to discipline errant councillors; and the establishment of local government tribunals which would be the arbiters on matters related to council's codes of conduct. Additionally, the Commission recommended the abolition of the regime of surcharging councillors who had committed acts of misconduct. However, even as the Commission was deliberating, there were instances of corruption in Glasgow, Paisley, Doncaster, Birmingham and Hull. The Nolan Commission's view that it could recover Gladstonian moral virtue failed to recognise the realities of corruption in the modern and the postmodern era. The causes of corruption as the studies of Glasgow, the operations of John Poulson and T. Dan Smith and Dame Shirley Porter show, were complex, often hidden and embedded in specific political situations and environments. These cases have shown that the corrupters – James Strain, Alexander Ritchie, T. Dan Smith, John Poulson and Dame Shirley Porter – had a range of particular skills to organise corrupt exchanges or transactions. Strain, Ritchie, Smith and Poulson were well versed in the skills of illegality. As members of organisations such as the Labour Party, trade unions and masons that cultivated friendship, generosity, fellowship and reciprocity, they were able to transfer those styles of behaviour into the illicit domain of corrupt transactions. Moreover, they were all prepared to take what they regarded as calculated risks whereby the moral costs of exposure were relatively low. They were only discovered by chance. Significantly, all these cases involved connivance by political parties. Alexander Ritchie was initially suspected in 1933, but he continued to be involved in corruption until 1941. Corruption in the north-east of England was tackled by Eddie Milne, the Labour MP for Blythe, but for his pains, he was deselected by his local constituency association. The cases of Glasgow and the north-east of England display a diffuse complicity between politicians, businessmen and public officials that created a culture of secrecy and collusion. In such circumstances, public goods can often be regarded as private property. This was certainly so with the Councillor Richard Embleton in Newcastle in the Second World War. Additionally, politicians are more inclined to be pragmatists than idealists, and pragmatism assists the corrupt as it fosters the complicity of silence. Politicians succeed by cultivating networks of support. These networks may be client structured, friendship based, or religiously or ethnically determined, and the cultivation of loyalty and support is derived from the exchange of favours which may be gifts disguised as loans or may be bribes or tribute.

The study of corruption in particular places is surely highly appropriate since the town and the city are and have been centres of economic exchange as well as nodal points of governance and political interaction. Studies of corruption in Italy, for example, demonstrate that the venues of corruption are the cities – Naples, Palermo, Catania and even Florence and Milan. In British cities, the practice of party group meetings, as quasi-whip systems, provides the opportunity for mediation and deals amongst like-minded collaborators which is remote from the public gaze. The arrangements for committee chair appointments provide council leaders with immense patronage particularly as those positions attract additional responsibility allowances. These confidential or secretive encounters are designed to achieve loyalty or obedience to the party line. They are essentially authoritarian in form and deferential to the leadership in result. There may well be dissent and particular councillors may stand up for their position, but it is at the risk of opprobrium from their fellows. The group meeting then promotes the culture of the deal or the bargain. Such transactions are similar to those of other organisations where loyalty and reciprocity override individual conscience: the masons, trade unions, chapels, self-help groups, immigrant associations based on ethnicity and religion, for example. Membership of such organisations constructs an identity separate from being a citizen of the state. Such an identity provides the opportunities of patronage, protection, mediation and the negotiation of business deals. This *milieu* is not dissimilar to that of a criminal fraternity where all these types of relationships and opportunities can be found.

Teaching moral virtues to those involved in political life is surely a difficult task. This is because the occurrence of corruption is at least a function of the structure of opportunities available to the would-be corrupt – drink licences, municipal contracts, expenses scams and building or road planning approvals – balanced against the moral costs of discovery. If there is substantial state involvement in the management of the economy or state promotion of building and construction projects, then the structure of opportunity moves in favour of the corrupter whether a politician or a businessman. In local government, if the councillor has been recruited from a low social class or status group, then de Tocqueville's dictum holds good as poorer men have their livings to make. Corruption can also occur where there is a polarised political culture and particularly where the balance of power produces paralysis which was certainly true in London with the confusion of obligations that existed between the GLC and the Boroughs. Corruption will occur not only where there is a blocked political system but also where clientism prevails and where the political class has accepted a culture of venality. The only check is the strength of civil society, which is strong and vibrant in British society but has become detached from urban political life, leaving the field to the party machines.

The phenomenon of the career politician also conspires against virtuous government. Nowhere was this more apparent than in Westminster in the Porter years. David Weeks, Barry Legg and Michael Dutt were willingly bullied by Dame Shirley Porter in order to promote their careers. Indeed, a political career may advance not just because an individual possesses particular technical abilities – finance or policy formation – but because he or she displays loyalty and conformism to the party line. The requisites of astuteness, pragmatism, guile and the ability to 'take out' an opponent are not too dissimilar to the qualities to be successful as part of a criminal fraternity. Progress for the career politician may also be secured by an ability to form links with wider society and to bring donations and contributions to party funds. Possession of a combination of these attributes can do much to promote a political career whether virtuous or venal.

In instances of corruption for 'noble cause' which might be the defence of T. Dan Smith or even Dame Shirley Porter, membership of a particular subculture may explain corruption. This may have been the case in Glasgow, Newcastle and certainly Belfast where the norms determining social relations disregard the state or its representatives as models of ethically governed behaviour. Further, where the state is weak, the value of being law abiding is low. This is not thought to be the case in British society although it may have been so in Northern Ireland and the cities of Belfast and Londonderry between 1922 and 1968. In such circumstances, the propensity for politicians, businessmen, bureaucrats and even the wider citizenry to be corrupt is great because the moral costs of discovery are low and the value of being ethical and law abiding is equally low.

The British case shows that the most effective check on corruption has been a strong and vigorous civil society and also a robust investigative journalism. However, it would seem that civil society in Britain has become detached from the conduct of urban politics and the energy of civil society and voluntary activity is directed elsewhere – conservation, the countryside and charity. Further, since the Local Government Act 2000, most local authorities and certainly those of the towns and cities have adopted a leader and cabinet arrangement; and some have adopted directly elected mayors. Such arrangements were intended to provide strong leadership, greater transparency and accountability which would be achieved by means of a scrutiny committee. There is evidence though that the scrutiny regime has not always worked as intended. Prevailing political culture where there is a large majority for one party over long periods of time has remained impervious to scrutiny and challenge; and in many authorities, individual members of scrutiny committees lack experience; and very often there is not a dedicated officer to support them. The experience of American cities would suggest that directly elected mayors do not provide a panacea for the elimination of corruption. In Britain, examples of corruption and poor governance persist. It is acknowledged however that a strong leader that cultivates an ethical environment and sets a tone of openness can ensure that council business can be conducted with propriety.

Appendix

Prosecution rates

In Britain, criminal statistics have been maintained for England and Wales since 1837. It is well known that criminal statistics of all types whether official or those produced by independent bodies should be handled with care. Such statistics are based on indictable offences and have been drawn from aggregate data produced by the police and the courts. Since 1982, the *British Crime Survey* has produced data on often unreported crime such as vandalism and rape although not on corruption. Local surveys suggest that routinely assembled criminal statistics as well as national survey data seriously under-record crime in general. There is no reason to suppose that corruption would be exceptional in this respect. Corruption might be considered to be a 'white collar' crime which has been considered to be an especially under-recorded crime. Nevertheless, prosecution rates are shown here derived from *House of Commons Parliamentary Papers* (HCPP).

Corruption Perception Index

The method used for the Corruption Perception Index involved the use of the British Library digital newspaper archive and the digital versions of *The Times*, *The Guardian* and *The Scotsman*. The overall British national picture has been derived from *The Times* and *The Guardian*. The British Library newspaper archive supplied information for Bristol and Leeds and *The Scotsman* was used for Glasgow. This provided some geographical spread, but there were a number of disadvantages. The composition of the newspapers altered over time; the time periods for particular newspapers were not always the same; and the provincial collection terminates by 1959. The Corruption Perception Index was created using a method developed by Edward Glaeser and Claudia Goldin.[1]

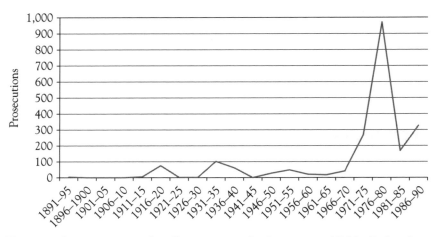

Figure 1   Prosecution rates for offences against the Corruption of Public Bodies Acts
(1889, 1906, 1916)

Sources: HCPP, *Reports of the Prosecution of Offences Acts 1890–1916*; HCPP, *Judicial Statistics 1917–29* (Cmd. Papers); HCPP, Home Office, *Criminal Statistics for England and Wales*, 1930–76 (Cmd. Papers); HCPP, *Reports of the Commissioner of Police for the Metropolis*, 1976–85; HCPP, *Reports of Her Majesty's Chief Inspector* 1986–89.

Cases processed under the Corruption Acts 1964–78 in Magistrates' Courts

	Proceeded against	Committed for trial
1889 Act	24	24
1906 Act	720	493
1933 Act	13	10
Total	757	527

Cases processed under the Corruption Acts 1964–78 in Crown Court

	Total for trial	Total guilty
1889 Act	24	23
1906 Act	52	45
1933 Act	13	10
Total	89	78

Figure 2   Cases proceeded against, 1964–78

Sources: Alan Doig, *Corruption and Misconduct in Contemporary British Politics* (London: Harmondsworth Penguin, 1984), pp. 387–401.

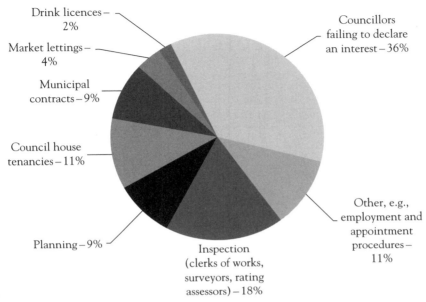

Figure 3   Types of corrupt transaction, 1964–78

Sources: Lord Redcliffe-Maud, *Prime Minister's Committee on Local Government Rules of Conduct*, 1974, Cmd., 5636; and Lord Salmon, *Royal Commission on Standards of Conduct in Public Life*, 1976, Cmd., 6524.

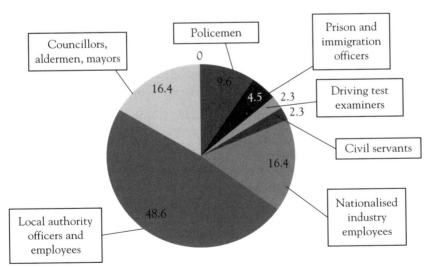

Figure 4   Occupations of individuals accused of corruption, 1964–72

Sources: Lord Redcliffe- Maud, *Prime Minister's Committee on Local Government Rules of Conduct*, 1974, Cmd., 5636.

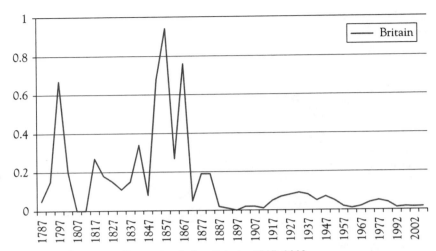

Figure 5   Corruption Perception Index, Britain, 1787–2002

Sources: Times Digital Archive 1785–1985; *The Guardian* 1990–2005.

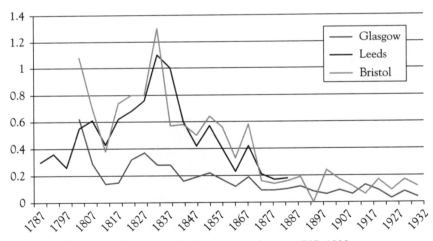

Figure 6   Corruption Perception Index, provincial cities, 1787–1932

Sources: British Library Newspaper Archive based on a sample from the *Glasgow Herald*, *Leeds Intelligencer*, *Leeds Mercury* and *Leeds Times*, *Western Daily Press*, *Bristol Mercury*.

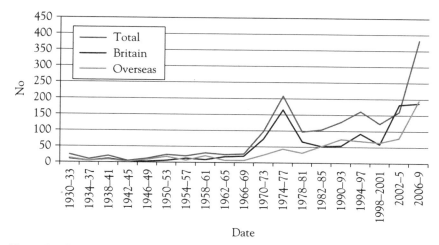

Figure 7   Corruption articles in *The Times* and *The Guardian*, 1930–2009

Sources: News articles specifically reporting on corruption cases 1930–2009 in *The Times* and *The Guardian*.

A simple word search for 'corruption' and 'bribery' was carried out, using the number of 'hits' to construct the index. Additionally, the word 'political' was used in the same fashion to provide a divisor or deflator. The convenience of the digital archives enabled a count of 'hits' on the three selected words. Thus, the calculation was:

$$CPI = \frac{(corruption + bribery)}{Political}$$

Or

$$I = \frac{(c+b)}{P}$$

Example:

$$I = \frac{(55+23)}{(72)}$$

$$I = 1.08$$

Note

1 Glaeser, E. and Goldin, G., *Corruption and Reform: Lessons from America's Economic History* (Chicago: University of Chicago Press, 2006).

Select bibliography

Abbreviations

Command Papers according to series: 1833–69 are numbered 1–4222
1870–99 are: C. 1–9550
1900–18 are: Cd. 1–9237
1919–56 are: Cmd. 1–9889
1956–86 are: Cmnd. 1–9927
1986– are: Cm. 1–

HCP: House of Commons Papers.
HO: Home Office.
NA: National Archives (formerly Public Record Office).

Official publications and reports

Bribery of Ministers of the Crown or Other Public Servants (1948), Cmd., 7616.
Committee of Public Accounts, Eighth Report (1993–94), HCP, 154.
The Conduct of Local Authority Business, HCP (1985–86), Cmd., 9797, 9798, 9800.
Glasgow Tribunal Inquiry (1933), Cmd., 4361.
Her Majesty's Chief Inspector of Constabulary (1985–88), HCP, 437, 32, 521, 449.
Home Office Criminal Statistics for England and Wales (1930–82), Cmd., 3581–8668.
Home Office Judicial Statistics (1919–29), Cmd., 3581–5595.
House of Commons, Metropolitan Board of Works (1889), C 5660.
Housing in Northern Ireland (1944), Cmd., 224.
Local Government in the Tyneside Area (1935), Cmd., 5402.
NA, H.O. 241/98, T. Dan Smith, written evidence to: *Standards of Conduct in Public Life* (1976), C458647.
NA, *The Cabinet Papers 1915–1982*.
Newcastle Tribunal Report (1944), Cmd., 6522.
Prime Minister's Committee on Local Government Rules of Conduct (1974), Cmd., 5636.
Raising Standards 2000, Cmd., 4759.
Report of Her Majesty's Commissioners Appointed to Inquire into the Revenues and Management of Certain Colleges and Schools (1864), 3288.

Report of the Committee on Intermediaries (1950), Cmd., 7904.

Reports of the Commissioner of Police for the Metropolis (1974–75), Cmd., 6068; (1975–76), Cmd., 6496; (1976–77), Cmd., 6821.

Reports of the Commissioners for Special Areas, England and Wales (1935–38), Cmd., 4957–5595.

Reports of the Commissioners for Special Areas, Scotland (1935–38), Cmd., 5089–905.

Royal Commission on Standards of Conduct in Public Life (1976), Cmd., 6524.

Select Committee on the Conduct of Members (1977), HCP, 1977.

Standards of Conduct in Public Life, First Report (1995), Transcripts of Evidence, Cmd., 2850-II.

Standards of Conduct in Public Life: Standards of Conduct in Local Government in England, Scotland and Wales, Third Report (1997–98), Cmd., 3702.

Tribunal on Ministry of Munitions: Alleged Instructions as to Documents (1921), Cmd., 1340.

Other public records

The Campaign for Social Justice in Northern Ireland, *Londonderry: One Man, One Vote* (Dungannon, 1965).

Hansard, House of Commons Debates (1900–96).

Newcastle Civil Defence Working Group of the Watch Committee, MD.NC/276/4-276/6 (22 February 1943–8 March 1950).

Peter Alldridge, 'Reforming bribery law', *Law Commission Consultation* (2008).

Poulson (a bankrupt) Re: ex-parte, Granada Television v. Maudling, 2 All ER 1020 (1976) 1 WLR 1023, SO1 JO734 (1976).

Poulson Papers, West Yorkshire Archive Service, Wakefield, C391/2/1–C391/2/211 (c.1955–70).

Stormont Papers: Parliamentary Debates of the Northern Ireland Government (1921–72).

Newspapers and magazines

Architectural Review
Belfast Telegraph
Bradford Telegraph and Argus
Bristol Mercury
Glasgow Herald
The Guardian
Hull Daily Mail
The Independent
The Irish Times
Leeds Intelligencer
Leeds Mercury
Leeds Times
Local Government Chronicle
Municipal Review
Northampton Chronicle and Echo
The Northern Echo
Nottingham Evening Post
The Observer

Private Eye
The Scotsman
The Spectator
The Times
Western Morning News
Western Daily Press
Woman's Own

Books

Aberbach, J. and R. Putnam, *Bureaucrats and Politicians* (London: Harvard University Press, 1981).

Alderman, G., *London Jewry and London Politics, 1889–1986* (London: Christopher Helm, 1989).

Banfield, E., *The Moral Basis of a Backward Society* (New York: Free Press, 1958).

Baron, S.W., *The Contact Man: The Story of Sidney Stanley and the Lynskey Tribunal* (London: Secker and Warburg, 1966).

Baston, L., *Reggie: The Life of Reginald Maudling* (Stroud: Sutton, 2004).

Bell, M., *A Very British Revolution: The Expenses Scandal and How to Save Our Democracy* (London: Icon Books, 2009).

Betjeman, J., *Collected Poems* (London: John Murray, 1979).

Bew, P., *Ireland: The Politics of Enmity 1789–2006* (Oxford: Oxford University Press, 2007).

Briggs, A., *Victorian Cities* (London: Harmondsworth Penguin, 1963).

Brown, A., D. McCrone and L. Paterson (eds.), *Politics and Society in Scotland* (Basingstoke: Macmillan, 1996).

Buckland, P., *Factory of Grievances: Devolved Government in Northern Ireland* (Dublin: Gill and Macmillan, 1979).

Budge, P. and C. O'Leary, *Belfast: An Approach to Crisis, A Study of Belfast Politics* (London: Macmillan, 1973).

Bull, M. and J. Newell, *Corruption and Contemporary Politics* (Cambridge: Polity Press, 2003).

Burke, P., *What Is Cultural History?* 2nd edn (Cambridge: Polity Press, 2008).

Burns, W., *New Towns for Old: The Technique of Urban Renewal* (London: Leonard Hill, 1963).

Butler, D. and G. Butler, *British Political Facts* (Basingstoke: Macmillan, 1974).

Checkland, S., *Scottish Banking: A History 1695–1973* (Edinburgh: John Donald, 1975).

Checkland, S., *The Upas Tree: Glasgow 1875–1975*, 2nd edn (Glasgow: University of Glasgow Press, 1981).

Clarke, M., *Fallen Idols: Elites and the Search for the Acceptable Face of Capitalism* (London: Junction, 1981).

Clarke, M. (ed.), *Corruption* (London: Pinter, 1983).

Colls, R. and W. Lancaster (eds.), *Newcastle-upon-Tyne: A Modern History* (Chichester: Phillimore, 2001).

Daunton, M. (ed.), *Cambridge Urban History of Britain*, vol. 3 (Cambridge: Cambridge University Press, 2000).

Della Porta, D. and Y. Meny (eds.), *Democracy and Corruption in Europe* (London: Pinter, 1997).

Della Porta, D. and A. Vanucci, *The Hidden Order of Corruption: An Institutional Approach* (Aldershot: Ashgate, 2012).

Devine, T., *Scottish Elites: Proceedings of the Scottish Historical Studies Seminar at the University of Strathclyde 1991–92* (Edinburgh: John Donald, 1994).

Devine, T., *The Scottish Nation 1707–2007* (London: Penguin, 2006).

Dimoldenberg, P., *The Westminster Whistle Blowers: Shirley Porter, Homes for Votes and Twenty Years of Scandal in Britain's Rottenest Borough* (London: Politico, 2006).

Doig, A., *Corruption and Misconduct in Contemporary British Politics* (London: Harmondsworth Penguin, 1984).

Donoghue, B. and G.W. Jones, *Herbert Morrison: Portrait of a Politician* (London: Weidenfeld and Nicolson, 1973).

Dunleavy, P., *The Politics of Mass Housing 1945–1975: A Study of Corporate Power and Professional Influence in the Welfare State* (Oxford: Clarendon Press, 1981).

Field, D., *A Survey of New Housing Estates in Belfast* (Belfast: Queens University Press, 1957).

Fitzwalter, R. and D. Taylor, *Web of Corruption: The Story of J.G.L. Poulson and T. Dan Smith* (London: Granada, 1981).

Fraser, W.H., *Scottish Popular Politics: From Radicalism to Labour* (Edinburgh: Polygon, 2002).

Fraser, W.H. and I. Maver (eds.), *Glasgow*, vol. II, 1839–1912 (Manchester: Manchester University Press, 1996).

Fukuyama, F., *Trust: The Social Virtues of Prosperity* (New Haven: Free Press, 1995).

Fukuyama, F., *State Building: Governance and World Order in the Twenty First Century* (London: Profile Books, 2005).

Fukuyama, F., *Origins of Political Order: From Pre-human Times to the French Revolution* (London: Profile Books, 2011).

Gillard, M., *Nothing to Declare: The Political Corruptions of John Poulson* (London: John Calder, 1980).

Gilmour, I., *Dancing with Dogma: Britain Under Thatcherism* (London: Simon and Schuster, 1992).

Ginsborg, P., *Italy and Its Discontents 1980–2001; Family, Civil Society and the State* (London: Penguin, 2001).

Glaeser, E., *The Triumph of the City: Why Urban Spaces Make Us Human* (Basingstoke: Pan Books, 2012).

Glaeser, E. and G. Goldin, *Corruption and Reform: Lesson's from America's Economic History* (Chicago: University of Chicago Press, 2006).

Goodson-Wickes, C., *The New Corruption* (London: Centre for Policy Studies, 1984).

Gordon, G. (ed.), *Regional Cities* (London: Harper and Row, 1986).

Goss, S., *Local Labour and Local Government: A Study in Changing Interests, Politics and Policy in Southwark from 1919 to 1982* (Edinburgh: Edinburgh University Press, 1988).

Gunn, S., *History and Cultural Theory* (Harlow: Longman, 2006).

Halsey, A.H., *Twentieth Century British Social Trends*, 3rd edn (Basingstoke: Macmillan, 2000).

Hampton, W., *Local Government and Urban Politics* (Harlow: Longman, 1999).

Harrison, B., *Transformation of British Politics 1860–1995* (Oxford: Clarendon Press, 1996).

Harrison, B., *Seeking a Role: The United Kingdom 1951–1970* (Oxford: Clarendon Press, 2009).

Harrison, B., *Finding a Role? The United Kingdom 1970–1990* (Oxford: Oxford University Press, 2010).

Heidenheimer, A., *Political Corruption: Readings in Comparative Analysis* (New York: Holt Rinehart and Winston, 1970).

Hennessey, P., *The Prime Minister: The Office and Its Holders Since 1945* (London: Allen Lane, 2000).

Hennock, P., *Fit and Proper Persons* (London: Edward Arnold, 1973).

Hosken, A., *Nothing Like a Dame: The Scandals of Shirley Porter* (London: Granta, 2006).

Huntington, S., *Political Order in Changing Societies* (New Haven: Yale University Press, 1969).

Joyce, P., *The Rule of Freedom: Liberalism and the Modern City* (London: Verso, 2003).

King, A. (ed.), *British Political Opinion 1937–2000: The Gallup Polls* (London: Politico, 2001).

Knox, W., *Scottish Labour Leaders 1918–1939* (Edinburgh: Mainstream Publishing, 1984).

Langford, P., *A Polite and Commercial People, England 1727–1783* (Oxford: Oxford University Press, 1989).

Laski, H., W.I. Jennings, E. Halevy, Sir I. Jennings and W.A. Robson, *A Century of Municipal Progress* (London: Allen and Unwin, 1935).

Lawrence, R.J., *The Government of Northern Ireland: Public Finance and Public Services 1921–1964* (Oxford: Clarendon Press, 1965).

Loughlin, M., *Half a Century of Municipal Decline: 1935–1985* (London: Allen and Unwin, 1985).

Lukes, S., *Power: A Radical View* (London: Palgrave, 2004).

Maclure, J., *Educational Documents: England and Wales 1816–1967* (London: Methuen, 1965).

Marriott, O., *Property Boom* (London: Hamish Hamilton, 1967).

Maver, I., *Glasgow* (Edinburgh: Edinburgh University Press, 2000).

McKinlay, A. and R.J. Morris, *The ILP on Clydeside 1893–1932: From Foundation to Disintegration* (Manchester: Manchester University Press, 1991).

Milne, E., *No Shining Armour* (London: John Calder, 1976).

Moore, J. and J. Smith (eds.), *Corruption in Urban Politics and Society, Britain 1780–1950* (Aldershot: Ashgate, 2007).

Morgan, K.O., *Labour in Power* (Oxford: Clarendon Press, 1984).

Morgan, K.O., *The People's Peace: British History 1945–1990* (Oxford: Oxford University Press, 1990).

Morris, R.J. and R.H. Trainor (eds.), *Urban Governance: Britain and Beyond Since 1750* (Aldershot: Ashgate, 2000).

Morrison, H., *How London Is Governed* (London: People's University Press, 1949).

Namier, L., *The Structure of Politics at the Accession of George III*, 2nd edn (London: Macmillan, 1957).

Neild, R., *Public Corruption: The Dark Side of Social Evolution* (London: Anthem, 2002).

Nuijten, M. and G. Anders, *Corruption and the Secret of the Law: A Legal Anthropological Perspective* (Aldershot: Ashgate, 2007).

O'Leary, C., *The Elimination of Corruption in British Elections 1886–1911* (Oxford: Clarendon Press, 1962).

Owen, D., *The Government of Victorian London 1855–1889: The Metropolitan Board of Works, Vestries and the City Corporation* (Cambridge, MA: Harvard University Press, 1982).

Porter, R., *London: A Social History* (London: Penguin, 1996).

Poulson, J., *The Price: The Autobiography of John Poulson, Architect* (London: Michael Joseph, 1981).

Putnam, R., R. Leonardi and Y.N. Rafaella, *Making Democracy Work: Civic Traditions in Modern Italy* (Princeton: Princeton University Press, 1994).

Rallings, C. and M. Thrasher, *Local Elections in Britain* (Plymouth: Local Government Chronicle Elections Centre, 1997).

Robson, W., *Local Government in Crisis* (London: Allen and Unwin, 1968).

Sampson, A., *The Anatomy of Britain Today* (London: Hodder and Stoughton, 1965).

Sandbrook, D., *White Heat: A History of Britain in the Swinging Sixties* (London: Abacus, 2006).

Searle, G., *Corruption in British Politics 1895–1930* (Oxford: Clarendon Press, 1987).

Shirlow, P. and B. Murtagh, *Belfast: Segregation, Violence and the City* (London: Pluto, 2006).

Simon, E., *Training for Citizenship* (London: Oxford University Press, 1935).

Smith, T.D., *Dan Smith: An Autobiography* (Newcastle: Oriel Press, 1970).

Smyth, J., *Labour in Glasgow 1896–1936: Socialism, Suffrage, Sectarianism* (East Linton: Tuckwell Press, 2000).

Sweet, R., *The English Town, 1680–1840* (Harlow: Longman, 1999).

Tiratsoo, N., *From Blitz to Blair* (London: Phoenix, 1997).

Turner, G., *The North Country* (London: Eyre and Spottiswoode, 1967).

Upsall, D., *Bradford City Council Behind Closed Doors* (London: Community Rights Project, 1984).

Vincent, D., *The Culture of Secrecy: Britain 1832–1998* (Oxford: Oxford University Press, 1998).

Waller, P., *Town, City and Nation* (Oxford: Oxford University Press, 1983).

Ward, R., *City-State and Nation: Birmingham's Political History c. 1830–1940* (Chichester: Phillimore, 2005).

Weber, M., *Economy and Society: An Outline of Interpretative Sociology* (New York: Bedminster Press, 1968).

White, J., *London in the Twentieth Century: A City and Its People* (London: Vintage, 2008).

Whitely, P., *Political Participation in Britain: The Decline and Revival of Civic Culture* (Basingstoke: Palgrave Macmillan, 2011).

Young, K., *Local Politics and the Rise of Party: The London Municipal Society and the Conservative Intervention 1894–1963* (Leicester: Leicester University Press, 1975).

Young, H., *The Hugo Young Papers: A Journalist's Notes from the Heart of Politics* (London: Penguin, 2008).

Young, K. and P. Garside, *Metropolitan London: Politics and Urban Change 1837–1981* (London: Edward Arnold, 1982).

Young, K. and N. Rao, *Local Government Since 1945* (Oxford: Blackwell, 1997).

Articles

Allan, C.M., 'The genesis of British urban re-development with special reference to Glasgow', *Economic History Review*, 18: 3 (1965), pp. 598–613.

Baugh, G.C., 'Government grants in aid of the rates', *Historical Research*, 65 (1992), pp. 215–33.

Boal, F. and D. Livingstone, 'Frontier in the city: ethnonationalism in Belfast', *International Political Science Review*, 5: 2 (1984), pp. 161–79.

Bourdieu, P., 'Re-thinking the state in genesis and structure in the bureaucratic field', *Sociological Theory*, 12: 1 (1994), pp. 1–18.

Brand, J., 'Party organisation and the recruitment of councillors', *British Journal of Political Science*, 3: 4 (1973), pp. 473–86.

Bull, P.J., 'The effects of redevelopment schemes of inner city manufacturing activity in Glasgow', *Environment and Planning*, 13 (1981), pp. 991–1000.

Byrne, D., 'Perspectives on T. Dan Smith: the disastrous effect of a liberal authoritarian modernizer', *North East Labour History Bulletin*, 28 (1994), pp. 19–26.

Challinor, R., 'Perspectives on T. Dan Smith: the youthful revolutionary', *North East Labour History Bulletin*, 28 (1994), pp. 15–18.

Chibnall, S. and P. Saunders, 'Worlds apart: notes on the social reality of corruption', *British Journal of Sociology*, 28 (1977), pp. 138–52.

Della Porta, D. and A. Pizzorno, 'Business politicians: reflections from a study of political corruption', *Journal of Law and Society*, 23: 1 (1996), pp. 73–96.

Doherty, P. and M. Poole, 'Ethnic residential segregation in Belfast, Northern Ireland 1971–1991', *Geographical Review*, 87 (1997), pp. 520–36.

Doig, A., 'Self-discipline and the house of commons: the Poulson affair in parliamentary perspective', *Parliamentary Affairs*, 32 (1979), pp. 248–67.

Doig, A., 'From Lynskey to Nolan: the corruption of British politics and public service', *Journal of Law and Society*, 23: 1 (1996), pp. 35–56.

Doig, A. and S. McIver, 'Corruption and its control in the developmental context: an analysis and selective review of the literature', *Third World Quarterly*, 20: 3 (1999), pp. 657–76.

Everett, J., D. Neu and A. Shiraz Rahaman, 'Global fight against corruption: a Foucaultion, virtues-ethics framing', *Journal of Business Ethics*, 65: 1 (April 2006), pp. 1–12.

Fennell, P. and P.A. Thomas, 'Corruption in England and Wales: an historical analysis', *International Society of Law*, 11 (1983), pp. 167–72.

Flyvbjerg, B., 'Habermas and Foucault: thinkers for civil society', *British Journal of Sociology*, 49: 2 (1998), pp. 210–33.

Fukuyama, F., 'Social capital and civil society', *IMF Working Paper No. 00/74* (2003).

Glaeser, E. and R. Saks, 'Corruption in America', *Working Paper No. 108821, National Bureau of Economic Research* (2004).

Goudie, A. and D. Stasavage, 'Corruption: the issues', *Working Paper No. 122, OECD Development Centre* (1997), pp. 1–53.

Jones, P., 'Re-thinking corruption in post-1950 urban Britain: the Poulson affair 1972–76', *Urban History*, 39: 3 (2012), pp. 510–28.

King, A., 'The rise of the career politician and its consequences', *British Journal of Political Science*, 11: 3 (July 1981), pp. 249–85.

Knox, W., 'Religion and the Scottish labour movement', *Journal of Contemporary History*, 23: 4 (1998), pp. 609–30.

Leonard, M., 'The politics of every-day living in Belfast', *The Canadian Journal of Irish Studies*, 18: 1 (July 1992), pp. 83–94.

Nelken, D. and M. Levi, 'The corruption of politics and the politics of corruption: an overview', *Journal of Law and Society*, 23: 1 (March 1996), pp. 1–17.

Oliver, D., 'Regulating the conduct of MPs: the British experience of combating corruption', *Political Studies*, 45 (1997), pp. 539–58.

Pacione, M., 'Housing policies in Glasgow since 1880', *Geographical Review*, 69: 4 (1979), pp. 395–412.

Paterson, I., 'Sectarianism and municipal housing allocation in Glasgow', *Scottish Affairs*, 39 (2002), pp. 39–53.

Pinto-Duschinsky, M., 'Corruption in Britain: the Royal Commission on Standards of Conduct in Public Life', *Political Studies*, 25: 2 (1977), pp. 274–84.

Robinton, M., 'The Lynskey tribunal: the British method of dealing with political corruption', *Political Science Quarterly*, 68 (1953), pp. 109–24.

Rodriguez, J., 'Ted Knight: interview', *Marxism Today*, 25 (1981), pp. 11–16.

Roodhouse, M., 'The Belcher affair and the Lynskey tribunal', *Twentieth Century British History*, 13: 4 (2002), pp. 384–411.

Rose-Ackerman, S. and S. Colazinqari, 'Corruption in a paternalistic democracy: lessons from Italy for Latin America', *Political Science Quarterly*, 113: 3 (1998), pp. 447–70.

Shapely, P., 'Civic culture and housing policy in Manchester 1951–1964', *Twentieth Century British History*, 15: 4 (2004), pp. 410–34.

Shapely, P., 'The entrepreneurial city: the role of local government and city centre re-development in post-war industrial English cities', *Twentieth Century British History*, 22: 4 (2011), pp. 498–520.

Sharpe, L.J., 'Elected representatives in local government', *British Journal of Sociology*, 13: 3 (1962), pp. 189–209.

Smyth, J.J., 'Resisting labour: unionists, liberals and moderates in Glasgow between the wars', *The Historical Journal*, 46: 2 (2003), pp. 375–401.

Weiler, P., 'The conservatives' search for a middle way in housing, 1951–64', *Twentieth Century British History*, 14: 4 (2003), pp. 360–90.

Theses and dissertations

Smith, E.R. *East End Jews: Politics 1918–1939: A Study in Class and Ethnicity* (University of Leicester, Unpublished PhD thesis, 1990).

Websites

British Newspaper Archive:
www.britishnewspaperarchive.co.uk
House of Commons Parliamentary Papers:
www.parlipapers.co.uk
Lexis Law Library:
www.lexisnexis.co.uk
Margaret Thatcher Foundation:
www.margaretthatcher.org
National Bureau of Economic Research NBER:
www.nber.org
Northern Ireland Conflict:
www.cain.ulst.ac.uk
OECD Library:
www.oecd-ilibrary.org
Oxford Dictionary of National Biography:
www.odnb.co.uk
Public Record Office of Northern Ireland:
www.proni.gov.uk
Red Clyde side: A History of the Labour Movement in Glasgow
www.gdl.cdlr.strath.ac.uk

Times Digital Archive:
www.gale.com
Transparency International:
www.transparency.org
World Bank:
www.worldbank.org/dataandresearch

Index